Island in the Crossroads

DR. JOHN HOPE FRANKLIN, Chairman of the History Department at the University of Chicago, has also taught at Brooklyn College, Fisk University, and Howard University. For the year 1962–63, he was William Pitt Professor of American History and Institutions at Cambridge University in England. He is the author of many books, including *From Slavery to Freedom, The Militant South, Reconstruction After the Civil War,* and *The Emancipation Proclamation.*

SHELLY UMANS is Director of the Center for Innovation, New York City Board of Education, and is a specialist in reading instruction and a member of the instructional staff of Teachers College, Columbia University. For more than ten years, she has been a consultant to many major urban school systems throughout the United States. She is the author of *New Trends in Reading Instruction, Designs for Reading Programs,* and co-author of *Teaching the Disadvantaged.*

DR. MARIA BRAU is assistant professor of history at Howard University in Washington, D.C., and co-author of another Zenith Book, *The Quiet Rebels.* Her grandfather, Salvador Brau, was the leading historian of Puerto Rico.

HERB STEINBERG studied with Moses Soyer while attending the High School of Music and Art in New York. He continued his training at the Tyler School of Fine Arts and, via a teaching fellowship at Kent State University, was awarded his master's degree in Fine Art. He has exhibited in national shows at the Brooklyn Museum, Pennsylvania Academy of Fine Art and the Better Institute.

The aim of Zenith Books is to present the history of minority groups in the United States and their participation in the growth and development of the country. Through histories and biographies written by leading historians in collaboration with established writers for young people, Zenith Books will increase the awareness of minority group members of their own heritage and at the same time develop among all people an understanding and appreciation of that heritage.

Other Outstanding Zenith Books

FOUR TOOK FREEDOM, By Philip Sterling and Rayford Logan. The lives of Harriet Tubman, Frederick Douglass, Robert Smalls, and Blanche K. Bruce.

A GLORIOUS AGE IN AFRICA, by Daniel Chu and Elliott Skinner. The story of three great African empires.

GREAT RULERS OF THE AFRICAN PAST, by Lavinia Dobler and William A. Brown, with special consultant Philip Curtin. Five African rulers who led their nations in times of crisis.

A GUIDE TO AFRICAN HISTORY, by Basil Davidson, revised and edited by Haskel Frankel. A general survey of the African past from earliest times to the present.

LIFT EVERY VOICE, by Dorothy Sterling and Benjamin Quarles. The lives of Booker T. Washington, W. E. B. Du Bois, Mary Church Terrell, and James Weldon Johnson.

PASSAGE TO THE GOLDEN GATE, by Daniel Chu and Samuel C. Chu. A history of the Chinese in America to 1910.

PIONEERS AND PATRIOTS, by Lavinia Dobler and Edgar A. Toppin. The lives of six Negroes of the colonial and revolutionary eras.

THE QUIET REBELS, by Philip Sterling and M. M. Brau. Four Puerto Rican leaders: José Celso Barbosa, Luis Muñoz Rivera, José de Diego, and Luis Muñoz Marín.

TIME OF TRIAL, TIME OF HOPE, by Milton Meltzer and August Meier. The history of the Negro in America from 1919 to 1941.

THE UNFINISHED MARCH, by Carol Drisko and Edgar A. Toppin. The Negro in the United States from Reconstruction to World War I.

WORTH FIGHTING FOR, by Agnes McCarthy and Lawrence Reddick. A history of the Negro in the United States during the Civil War and Reconstruction.

Island in the Crossroads

The History of Puerto Rico

M. M. Brau, Ph.D.

Illustrated by Herbert Steinberg

ZENITH BOOKS
DOUBLEDAY & COMPANY, INC., GARDEN CITY, NEW YORK
1968

Contents

Island in the Crossroads

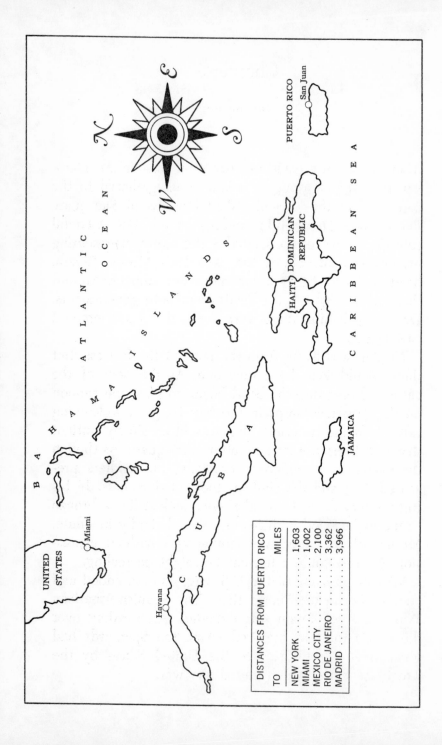

DISTANCES FROM PUERTO RICO

TO	MILES
NEW YORK	1,603
MIAMI	1,002
MEXICO CITY	2,100
RIO DE JANEIRO	3,362
MADRID	3,966

Chapter 1

Borinquen

About noon on a clear and beautiful day—it was October 18, 1898—a group of solemn men gathered in the courtyard of the ancient Palace-Fortress of San Juan, Puerto Rico. There, in his uniform, stood Major General John R. Brooke, of the United States Army, representing his government. There, too, was Luis Muñoz Rivera, head of Puerto Rico's autonomous government. Around these leaders gathered officials from both governments. Drawn up behind them were the ranks of soldiers and cavalrymen.

No flag was flying from the mast at the fortress, but there would soon be a new one. As the bells of the cathedral rang out, the band began to play, the cannon on the American ships in the bay let go a welcoming salvo, and the American flag was lifted slowly until it flew at full mast. A silence fell on the square. As though they were at a religious ceremony, the soldiers presented arms and the civilians took off their hats. In his full military dress, General Brooke looked like a bronze statue as he stood with his arm raised rigidly in salute. Muñoz Rivera's face was somber and without expression. No one could tell what he might be feeling.

With this raising of the U.S. flag, one era ended and another began for Puerto Rico. The Spanish-American War was over. Spain was defeated. After ruling over the island for four hundred years, the Spaniards had given over Puerto Rico to the United States by the Treaty of Paris, which ended the war.

Later that afternoon, long after everyone had left the courtyard, a Puerto Rican who had been an artillery officer in the Spanish Army walked slowly through the calm and peaceful streets of San Juan. He was Captain Angel Rivero. For forty-eight hours he had been an important man in this city. Like so many of his countrymen that day, he needed to sit quietly and think things over. Relaxed on a bench in the plaza, he went over in his mind once more the events of the last few days.

Most of the Spanish forces had left, and Captain Rivero had been placed in command of the remaining garrison. That made him the last Spanish officer to be charged with military duties in Puerto Rico. At ten-thirty that morning he had handed over the fortress of San Cristóbal to the American troops, and he would never enter there again. He had collected all the Spanish flags and put them in a cedar chest. In a few days he would give them to his former superior officer, General Ortega, who would take them back to Spain. The general would be going back to his own country. Captain Rivero would remain on the island that had always been his home, and he could not help wondering what would happen to him, and to his native country.

"Their lips silent but their hearts weeping," it was said of the Puerto Ricans at that moment. They shared the captain's uneasy feelings. Those who knew the history of their island, however, remembered that in all its long life, it had always been challenged to survive. And it had always survived. In their hearts they knew it would survive now.

Their story of survival begins in 1493 with Christopher Columbus' second voyage to the New World. His first trip, the year before, had been adventurous enough.

It had ended with the discovery which made the name of Columbus famous from that day to this. On the first voyage he had landed on Cuba and on Hispaniola, as he called the island which is now the Dominican Republic and Haiti. Queen Isabella and King Ferdinand were so pleased with the reports he brought back to Spain that they gave him seventeen ships to make another expedition.

This second voyage left Spain in September. Early in November, following mostly the route of 1492, Columbus approached an island he had not seen before. He called it Guadalupe, but when his small boats landed on the sandy beach, he found only empty villages. All the inhabitants had fled. They had left behind some women and children who were prisoners from a raid on a nearby island. These captives, thankful to be rescued, told Columbus through sign language, and by pointing, where they had come from and how to get there. Following their directions, he set sail and on November 16 sighted the mountains of the island that is now Puerto Rico.

As the ships approached the southwestern coast, the captive women whom Columbus was taking back home cried out excitedly, "Borinquen! Borinquen!" when they saw their native land. Borinquen (or Boriquén) was the Indian name for the island. The women were so glad to see Borinquen again that rather than wait for the small boats to be put down, they jumped overboard, swam the short distance to shore, and disappeared into the lush green vegetation. Watching them go, Columbus could easily understand why they were in such a hurry. It was not only because they wanted to see friends and relatives again, but it was also plain that they were overjoyed to see their beautiful island once more, hanging like an emerald between sea and sky.

The ships then slowly sailed along the western coast until they reached a splendid beach somewhere on the northwestern tip of the island. It was there that Columbus himself landed with his men. No one knows the exact day, but it is celebrated officially on November 19. After landing, Columbus sent scouts inland who soon returned to report they had found only a deserted village. For two more days, the ships stayed on, as though the navigator and his men could not bring themselves to leave so much beauty. Many different flowers bloomed about them, and huge trees were laden with fruit. So many clear springs bubbled up from the earth that the sailors had no trouble filling up their water casks for the next part of the voyage.

Before he left, Columbus named the island San Juan Bautista, and except for the Panama Canal Zone, it is today the only place Columbus landed which is under the U.S. flag.

The great navigator never returned, but there was a young soldier in his company who longed to come back to the island, and did. Juan Ponce de León lived for fifteen years in Hispaniola. There he became so important a man that he was given the southern part of the island to govern. But always he thought of "the beautiful island" he had first seen with Columbus, and in 1508 he asked for permission from the King and Queen to explore Borinquen. It was granted.

With twenty men, Ponce landed once more on the same beach he had explored with Columbus. This time he had a valuable ally of his own, his friend Juan González. Juan not only had learned to speak the Indian language, but also to disguise himself so that he looked like an Indian. He went alone to a nearby village, where Ponce hoped he would be able to make friendly contact with the inhabitants.

These villagers were Arawak Indians, who also lived on the other islands of this group, which was known as the Antilles. They were strong, good-looking, peaceful, intelligent, and brave in war. At that moment they had need to be brave because another Indian tribe, the Caribs, were trying to take over Borinquen. The Caribs —the Caribbean was named for them—were warlike. They came from the part of South America now called Venezuela. Not content with their own country, they had begun moving northward from island to island, conquering each one as they went. The Caribs had already taken Guadalupe, and the women who guided Columbus had been their prisoners, captured during a raid on Borinquen.

According to their custom, the Arawaks had divided Borinquen into districts, each ruled by a lord called a *cacique,* and a Supreme Cacique commanded them all. Quite a few towns in Puerto Rico still bear the names of caciques who ruled when Ponce arrived—Caguas, Orocovis, Humacao, Arecibo and Canóbanas, among others.

The district leaders were supported by the next level of the population, the warriors, who were the nobility of the island. Below these two groups were the rest of the population, poor people who did the work in peacetime and became soldiers whenever there was a war. The women were thought to be as important as the men. They had to do their share of the work, and sometimes they rose to the rank of cacique.

Men and women alike had a simple religion. They believed in one Supreme Being or god, who ruled over other gods, some good and some evil. One of these evil gods was called Huracán. He was thought to be responsible for the violent storms which often swept the islands, and that is why such storms are called "hurricanes" today.

González had learned all these facts about the Arawaks. He knew how they organized their communities, so he asked at once to be taken to the local cacique, Aymamón, who agreed to receive the visitors. González then went back to get Ponce and the other men.

Aymamón welcomed them with a great feast, which pleased Ponce. Since the Arawaks seemed friendly, he decided to use them as much as he could. First he needed more information.

"Do you have other bays as splendid as this one?" he asked.

"Yes," Aymamón answered, and added, "I am willing to provide you with guides so you can see the whole island."

With the help of these guides, Ponce finally reached the territory ruled over by the Supreme Cacique, Agüeybaná, who also received him with the greatest friendliness. Encouraged by all this, Ponce assured Agüeybaná that his intentions were peaceful. That was more necessary than he knew. The Arawaks had been badly treated by the Spaniards in the neighboring islands, and the Supreme Cacique had some reason to doubt his visitor's promises. Nevertheless, the two men made a pact of friendship.

This required a formal ceremony. While it was going on, Ponce's greedy eyes fell upon a round gold disk

Columbus discovered Puerto Rico and one of his men, Ponce de
Leon, returned to settle on the island.

hanging from a chain around Agüeybaná's neck. It was the symbol of his authority.

"Is that metal to be found on this island?" he asked.

Agüeybaná did not answer directly. He took Ponce by the hand and led him to the edge of a nearby river, whose banks glittered with deposits of gold. The Indians called the river the Coayuco; now called the Yauco.

Ponce could hardly believe his eyes. But he had seen enough to convince him that the Spaniards must own this island. It was almost enough just to know that the soil was so fertile it could support the lush green plants he saw everywhere he looked. The valleys between the mountains would make rich pasture land as well. And now gold!

Wisely, Ponce decided that it would be best to take advantage of the Indians' obvious friendliness. They looked at the Spaniards as though they were superior beings. As a result, with the help of Agüeybaná, Ponce built a small stone fortress, two farmhouses, and a short but adequate dock. Then he sailed back to Hispaniola, looking for settlers, but he carefully invited Agüeybaná to make the trip too, then or later. The Supreme Cacique soon afterward did come to Hispaniola, where Ponce showed him around the Spanish settlements and introduced him to all the important officials.

So the colony started with good feelings on both sides. The cacique's good will delighted the Spaniards, and he in turn could not help being impressed by what the Spaniards had already done. It was no hard task, therefore, for Ponce to recruit settlers. Three months after Agüeybaná's visit, a hundred men went back to Borinquen with Ponce, and a new Spanish colony began.

Chapter 2

The Conquistadores' Conquest

With the establishment of Ponce's colony, Puerto Rico became a part of Spain's new empire in the Indies. King Ferdinand himself recognized that fact in 1511 by granting the island a coat of arms, the first given to a colony in the New World. It is still in use today as the official seal of Puerto Rico.

To be a part of the Spanish Empire in those days simply meant that Spain began to rule over the Indians and their lands by right of conquest, peaceful or otherwise. In Borinquen there were no Puerto Ricans yet, only Arawaks and Spaniards, but how they stood in relation to each other was not yet decided.

Not all Spaniards could agree about what the position of the defeated Indians was supposed to be. There were angry arguments about the "rights of the conqueror" and the "rights of the conquered."

Different men had different answers to the problem. Some said, "We Spaniards have no more rights over the Indians than the Indians would have over the Spaniards if *they* had discovered Spain." And others agreed, "All men are created by God, and the Indians are creatures of God, therefore they are the equals of the Spaniards and ought to have the same rights." The Spaniards, these people said, should let the Indians carry on peaceful trade and should preach the Gospel to them. In return, the Spaniards should not attack the Indians unless they were attacked first, and should never force them to be servants, or slaves.

When Puerto Rico became part of Spain's new empire, the King of Spain gave the island a coat of arms.

Those who disagreed would say, "Before we came, the Indians themselves had set up empires over other Indians and made slaves and servants out of the defeated ones. Now we have conquered these empires, and because we are the strongest it is only fitting that we rule over them."

Then there were always those who took a middle position. "As matters stand, these Indians are backward," they said. "We ought to rule over them kindly and educate them until they think and act like Spaniards. When that time comes, but only then, should they be given equal rights."

Of course this was an argument that had been going on since the beginning of history. Usually those who lived in conquered nations had no rights except those the conquerors might choose to give them. It was not until the Spaniards had begun to conquer a part of the New World that doubts began to rise about whether this was right. The idea of justice for all men, wherever they might be, was beginning to be talked about.

The Indians usually had the Spanish kings on their side. By the end of the 1500s, laws had been passed in Spain which made the Indians subjects of the Crown. They had the same rights as Spanish subjects. On the other hand, nobody seemed to worry about the rights of the African slaves in the colonies. The Spaniards had what seemed to them like a good argument for doing nothing about these slaves. They had been bought, so it was said, from African rulers, in a commercial deal. But this sale did not make the slaves subjects of the Spanish King. If anything, it left them still subjects of the African rulers who had sold them. By the act of selling them, the Spaniards said, these rulers had deprived the slaves of any rights they might have enjoyed before.

The good intentions of the King and his advisers concerning the Indians were not nearly enough. The Spanish Empire was very large, stretching into many parts of what was then known of the world. Since it took so long for news and orders to flow from one part to the other, the government could not control everything that happened everywhere in the Empire. It was no secret, even to the King, that the King's laws were not always obeyed.

Why they were not was easy enough to see. While the King and his ministers debated these questions in the far-off comfort of the capital, Spain's hardfisted fighting men, the Conquistadores, were engaged in the real and often bloody business of conquest. These men of action thought they had a right to make the laws suit themselves. After all, they had crossed the ocean in ships never planned or built for journeys so long and dangerous. After surviving all kinds of hardships, they had reached unknown lands which had to be charted and explored. They had struck off into the wilderness, clearing paths through the dense jungles, navigating the most dangerous rivers with primitive equipment. Once away from the tiny settlements which clung to the edge of the continent, they had no more contact with these places and could expect no help if they were in trouble. And there was always trouble. From the start they knew they were going to be hopelessly outnumbered by the Indians, many of whom were unfriendly.

Most Conquistadores never expected to come back alive, but if they did, they wanted to be paid well for their labors. As one of them said, "I went to the Indies to serve God and King, to give light to those who were in darkness, and to grow rich, as all men desire to do."

The first Spanish governor of Puerto Rico, Ponce de León, was one of this breed of men. After he returned to the island with the agreement of his friend Agüeybaná, he placed most of the Indian population under the protection of his settlers. At first the Indians and settlers worked together. The settlers taught the Indians how to read and write, and converted many to Christianity. In return, the Spaniards expected the Indians to work for them, especially mining gold. It pleased the Spaniards to see that hard work was not a new thing to the Indians. For hundreds of years they had labored for their caciques and warriors.

Slowly, however, the Indians began to see a difference between the old ways and the new. They grew angry at having to work such long hours. Some of the settlers treated them badly, which they naturally resented. Agüeybaná took their complaints to Ponce, and the governor tried to please the cacique as much as he could. But then Agüeybaná died in 1510, and his young brother Guaybaná took his place.

The new chief was a different kind of man. He saw no reason to keep on friendly relations with Ponce. More and more Indians were dying of disease and exhaustion from hard labor. Guaybaná had to deal directly with Cristóbal de Sotomayor, who was Ponce's representative in the southern part of the island. But neither from him nor from Ponce could he obtain any promises of relief from the horrible conditions he had seen for himself.

Now the Indians began a passive resistance to Spanish

demands. They simply dragged their heels and quietly refused to co-operate. There was yet no thought of violence, because it was widely believed among the Indians that the Spaniards lived forever, like the gods. One day, however, the Indians captured a young soldier who was traveling alone. They held him under water in a river until he was dead. That was all the proof they needed. Spaniards could be killed, like other men. Guaybaná called the caciques and warriors to a secret war council at the ancient seat of Indian power near the Yauco River. It was the same place Agüeybaná had first pointed out the gold deposits to Ponce.

Juan González, Ponce's old friend, who so often wandered among the Indians in disguise overheard talk about the war council. He hurried to warn Cristóbal de Sotomayor of possible trouble. Sotomayor soon had a second warning, from Guaybaná's sister, Guanina, who had fallen in love with him and feared he might be killed.

Disguised as an Indian warrior, González attended the secret meeting. What he heard was even worse than he may have expected. Guaybaná stood in the center of the war council and explained his plan. "Each among you," he commanded the caciques, "will kill that Spaniard to whom he has been entrusted. I myself will give the example by killing Cristóbal de Sotomayor. You will know when the deed is done when torches light the sky atop our mountains. Then will you go. Then will you kill."

Turning to the warriors, he went on: "At the same signal, you shall burn the settlements and destroy all other Spaniards who yet live." The war dances began, and while the drums were beating, Juan González slipped away in the darkness to tell Sotomayor what he had heard.

Listening to González, the Spanish leader knew he must warn Ponce de León at once, but the governor was at that moment in the settlement of Caparra, to the north. This meant that Sotomayor had to cross the island from south to north, passing through the territories of hostile Indians. Ignoring the risk, he announced the next day to everyone, including Guaybaná, that he was leaving on a trip to Caparra. As a Spanish Conquistador, it would have been against his honor to leave in secrecy, which might be thought of as a sign of cowardice. Guanina went with him, for she refused to let her handsome Spaniard go alone into danger.

As the little company pushed its way through the jungle, Juan González fell back far to the rear of the others, thinking to act as a guard. But he did not hear the movement of Indian bodies slipping through the underbrush around him. When three arrows flew silently through the air into his body, he fell without a sound, unable to give warning to his friends who marched ahead. Guaybaná and two hundred warriors, who had shadowed the Spaniards for some time, then surrounded and attacked the rest of them. Desperately Guanina tried to shield Don Cristóbal, crying out to her brother for mercy, but Guaybaná was pitiless and shot an arrow through her heart. Sotomayor and his companions fought back but the odds were much too great. In an hour, they were all dead.

All, that is, except for Juan González. The arrows had not killed him after all. Recovering a little when the Indians had gone by, he struggled to his feet and climbed a tree, where he hid and watched the warriors

who had come back for his body. When they gave
up the search in puzzlement, González crawled away
and somehow managed to reach Caparra to warn Ponce.
There was no time to send warnings elsewhere.

Before they knew it, the Spaniards found themselves
caught in a flaming rebellion. All over the island Spanish houses were burning. The settlers formed a circle
with the women and children in the center, and fought
their Indian attackers through a long and bloody night.
Next day the settlers began a slow retreat toward Caparra, which the survivors reached in a few days of
continuous rear-guard action.

When they had arrived, Ponce de León counted his
garrison. He had 120 men, some of them wounded, many
unskilled in war. Nor would there be time enough to
get reinforcements from Hispaniola. On the other side,
the cacique Guaybaná faced him with at least 11,000
warriors, according to Juan González's report. Ponce had
no way of knowing how many men the other caciques
had been able to gather together.

Faced with these odds, the Spanish commander decided not to wait for the Indians to descend on Caparra,
which had no defenses. He would attack!

With a pitiful army of only eighty men, he marched
toward the Yauco area, where he knew the Indians were
celebrating a feast. Arriving at night, he launched a
surprise attack at once, with a result that must have
astonished as well as pleased him. At the attack, the
Indians woke up in terror, thinking in their superstitious
fear that the Spaniards they had killed had come back
to life seeking revenge. They fled in utter confusion,
while the Spaniards hacked away at them in the darkness, killing hundreds.

But that was only a small part of the Indian force. When Guaybaná, camped a distance away, heard the news of this massacre, he assembled a huge army and prepared to counterattack. Ponce knew that to fight back was hopeless, but he had no other choice.

Again using their circle formation, the Spaniards fought off wave after wave of attackers until Guaybaná, in desperation, led his warriors himself in a final charge. As they came on, a young Spanish soldier fired a fatal shot at Guaybaná. When their leader fell dead, the Indians reeled back in dismay and confusion. Then this powerful army fled, leaving the handful of Spaniards victorious.

The fate of Puerto Rico was decided on that historic day. The Spaniards had won, and the insurrection of 1511, as it is known in Puerto Rican history, was crushed. Later some of the caciques and their warriors surrendered to Ponce. Others escaped to neighboring islands, joining forces with the Caribs and continuing to make stealthy raids along the coast. When the laws for the protection of Indians began to be enforced, the majority of those who remained went to live in the mountains. Only about a thousand were left in the service of the Spaniards.

The story of Ponce and the Indians was repeated again and again in the New World. Indians and Spaniards fought each other, but they also mingled. Often they intermarried, and a new combination of heritages was created. In Borinquen, almost half the Spanish settlers were married to Indian women.

So the personality we call "Puerto Rican" began to develop. The name itself came from the "rich port" in the northeast, next to which Ponce had built Caparra.

The town later built near that site was known as the "City of the Rich Port." Gradually the name of San Juan which Columbus had given to the island was applied only to that city, and it became the capital. Puerto Rico, the original name of the town, was used to mean the entire island.

Ponce de León did not live to see all this happen. As a soldier born and bred, he grew bored with his job as governor. He became tired of filing written reports and arguing points of law with the higher authorities in Spain. He yearned to explore new lands. Especially he wanted to search for the isle of Biminí. He had heard from Indian legends that a miraculous fountain existed on this island which would bring back youth. Ponce was too practical a man to believe that a "fountain of youth" really existed. What attracted him was the part of the legend which told of the great gold deposits in the area around the fountain. He wanted to find out if that part of the story was true.

While he was hunting for the "gold of Biminí," the first governor of Puerto Rico also became one of the first Europeans to explore what is now the United States. Ponce de León discovered Florida, but instead of the gold he sought, he found death at the hands of hostile Indians. They wounded him in the leg—a wound which developed gangrene and led to his death in 1521.

It was the end of a remarkable, adventurous career, and the end, too, of the first episode in Puerto Rico's history. The colony Ponce left behind faced hard days ahead.

Almost half the Spanish settlers were married to Indian women and lived in small villages.

Chapter 3

Ups and Downs

For a time the colony of Puerto Rico was one of the Spanish Crown's most prized possessions. Spaniards of good family, with their wives and children, settled on the island. During the first fifty years of the sixteenth century, however, the colony began to go slowly downhill, for many different reasons.

For one thing, the Spaniards soon mined out the gold deposits. By 1540, the amount of metal taken from the ground was very little, and it was not long after that mining activity ended entirely. This meant that a man could no longer get rich quickly. Thus one of the chief reasons for attracting and holding colonists on the island disappeared, and the future of Puerto Rico depended on settlers. It was important for those who were not miners to stay and cultivate the soil. If they did, the island could become a thriving farming community.

But these settlers were men of peace. They had been happy to let the Conquistadores fight the Indians. They depended on the soldiers to stay and protect them even if the gold was gone. After all, how could anyone settle down to farming, they asked, if he might wake up any morning to find his lands burned and his cattle mutilated or killed?

There were already many victims of raids by Indians trying to drive the Spanish out of their islands. Pedro Mejía, for one, a hard-working farmer, who was married to a beautiful Indian girl named Luisa; both of them were killed one night in a Carib raid. And there was

Sancho de Aragón, a Conquistador turned farmer. He hoped to survive because of his famous watchdog, Becerrillo. This dog had defended his master so bravely during several Indian raids that the government had given the animal a sum equal to a soldier's pay. But the relentless Caribs came again. This time Sancho had almost been taken prisoner, and Becerrillo had died defending him.

Sancho was lucky, at that. To be taken prisoner by the Caribs could be worse than a sentence of death. Everyone knew how Don Cristóbal de Guzmán had been captured, along with some of his servants. When the women among them had been found later, abandoned, they told horrible tales of torture, slow death, and cannibalism. The Franciscan friars, peacefully building a small church, had been attacked. Only three managed to escape.

If a farmer was lucky enough to avoid such disasters, there were always hurricanes to fear. One of them in 1527 had destroyed all the crops in a single devastating day. Another year, 1530, brought two hurricanes, one in July and another in August, which left scarcely a single house standing and totally ruined the crops.

Even if a man survived hostile Indians and hurricanes, he had to face the hard problem of trying to find someone to help him with his work. It was very difficult to find Indians who would take the job. African slaves had been brought to Puerto Rico, but they rebelled against their masters, and fought along with the Caribs against these Spanish settlers. In any case, many men trying to start a farm, who saw their crops destroyed over and over again, could not afford to buy slaves.

It was no wonder, then, that the settlers began to

listen to visitors stopping at the island on their way
to Mexico and Peru. After hearing about the money
to be made in those places, many a ragged settler prayed,
"May the Lord take me to Perú!" An increasing number
refused to wait for the Lord's help, but boarded ship
and sailed with the visitors, so that the island was soon
in danger of being without a population. There came
a time when a ship on its way to Perú, anchored in
the bay of San Juan, was besieged by crowds of des-
perate settlers. They tried to reach it by any means
they could find. Those who were not lucky enough
to have canoes tried to swim for it, and the alarmed
governor sent his men after the colonists who were attempting to leave and forcibly brought them back.

This action outraged the would-be emigrants. They
protested so loudly in letters and petitions sent to
Spain that the Crown had to declare as a matter of
principle that settlers could not be stopped from leaving the island if they wished to go.

As soon as news of this decree reached Puerto Rico,
hundreds of settlers began leaving. This shocked and
alarmed the Spanish government. It had no idea its
ruling would be so popular. Wisely, this time, the government did not try to keep the colonists on the island
by force. Instead it made an attempt to do something
about the conditions which made the settlers want to
leave. To provide protection against Indian raids, money
was sent to build fortresses in Puerto Rico. Work started
on Morro Castle, which still stands guard at the entrance
to San Juan Bay.

The Spanish government took other steps to help
the colonists. Spain sent construction materials to build
ships which would guard the coast from Indian raiders.

Taxes paid to the Crown were done away with until the emergency was over. Farmers were granted loans, on good terms, to promote the cultivation of sugar. The government also increased the garrison of soldiers and sent out new farmers, with their families, to replace those who had left for Mexico and Perú.

Some of these steps, however, proved to be not as helpful as they sounded. For one thing, part of the money meant to be used for building forts had to be used instead to help pay for labor to build the ships. Soldiers also had to be paid, and even if the tax collections had been kept up, there would still not have been enough money for the new garrison.

In this financial squeeze, the Crown arranged to have an annual subsidy of two million pesos sent to Puerto Rico. It was to come from another of its colonies, Mexico, which had a surplus in its budget. This subsidy was called the Situado. It quickly became the chief source of income for the government of the island.

Unfortunately, more often than not the Situado did not arrive on schedule, and the professional soldiers had to get along on whatever their civilian neighbors could spare. Many soldiers had to be excused from guard duty, consequently, because they did not have enough clothes to wear. "It breaks one's heart to look at them," a governor wrote sadly to his superiors in Spain.

Nor did the sugar industry prosper, in spite of loans. The labor problem remained stubbornly unsolved. And the hurricanes, smashing through the island with depressing frequency, cut down the growth of crops to a minimum.

It was true that there were fewer and fewer Indian raids, but another, perhaps even a greater danger threat-

French, Dutch, and English pirates constantly attacked settlements along the coast of Puerto Rico.

ened these unlucky settlers. Although Puerto Rico was not a rich island, its location made it highly important to the defense of the Spanish Caribbean. As a result other European countries interested in acquiring an empire or lands of their own in the New World encouraged attacks on it. The coast settlements were constantly under attack by French, Dutch, and English pirates. One of them, the little town of San Germán, was sacked and destroyed by the French three times within fifteen years.

It was the English, however, who were giving the Spaniards the most trouble, as an undeclared war continued to boil and bubble between the two nations. Elizabeth I, the English Queen, unofficially encouraged private ships to raid Spanish galleons, and to loot various Spanish outposts. Some of the commanders of these raiding ships (they came to be known as "seadogs") were famous men in their own time, as they are still today. Probably the most famous was Sir Francis Drake, a captain so bold and notorious that Spanish mothers frightened their children with his name.

The Caribbean first saw Drake in 1585. He sailed his ships into Santo Domingo and took the capital of Hispaniola, one of the largest cities in the Spanish Empire and a well-fortified town. Drake destroyed it so completely that it was never able to recover. Later he raided Cartagena as well, but there fever swept his army and did what Spanish guns could not do, leaving him with only 800 men out of a force of 2300.

Ten years later, in 1595, he was back again, this time with no mere raid in mind. He meant to conquer the West Indies, and he had a bold plan outlined to do it, which included as one of its key parts the capture of Puerto Rico.

But the Spaniards had not been inactive in the ten years between Drake's visits. Constant appeals to Spain after the first raid had resulted in more troops and a military engineer being sent to Puerto Rico, where they helped to go on building the battlements of Morro Castle. Many citizens also volunteered their help. Having no idea when Drake, or other raiders, might come again, they worked around the clock to finish the fortification. By 1591 they had completed it. A fortress finally defended the city of San Juan.

That was the surprise waiting for Drake when he returned, thinking to fall upon the defenseless community. The English commander had decided that surprise would be the best strategy. Just before dawn on November 22, 1595, the English fleet approached the island, with muffled oars. Complete silence had been ordered as the ships crept closer and closer into San Juan Harbor. Drake had no idea that a fort high enough to observe him now overlooked the harbor. On its battlements an alert sentry caught the shadowy passage of the ships in the morning fog. Although he could not tell what flag they flew, he knew this silent approach could only mean an enemy. Without waiting to see any more, he shouted the warning. Many of the soldiers were only just waking up, but they responded instantly to the alarm and rushed to man the shore batteries.

Meanwhile, Drake was in his cabin aboard his flagship, talking with two of his officers. He was so sure of success that he felt it unnecessary to be on deck. Suddenly the world was upside down. A cannon shot burst through the wall of the cabin, knocking him from his seat. He staggered to his feet, shocked and stunned, and saw his two companions lying dead in the wreckage.

Taking command, Drake withdrew and placed his ships in a position to lay siege to the port. For two days the English cannon bombarded the town, trying to move in under the fire close enough to land. But the island's defenders kept them at a distance with an answering barrage which went on day and night. On the morning of the twenty-fifth, Drake decided that an attack could not succeed. He ordered his ships to withdraw. The defenders, who were expecting another attempt that day, raised a cheer of triumph and relief as they saw the English ships leaving. The shouts of victory echoed from the soldiers at their gunposts to the civilians who were loading ammunition, and on to the women and children who were praying for this moment of triumph. The defenders had reason to be proud. Only a handful of men, they had turned back England's mightiest seadog.

It was only the first of a series of disasters for Drake. What the Spaniards had begun, mosquitoes and the climate completed. The English commander died shortly afterward, off Puerto Bello.

Queen Elizabeth was not ready to give up the idea of conquering Puerto Rico, in spite of Drake's failure. In 1598, she sent another commander on the same mission. This famous captain, Lord Cumberland, was determined that he would not make Drake's mistake all over again. He had a different plan. To avoid the Morro Castle's shore batteries, he landed his men on an unguarded beach, out of sight of San Juan, and by a forced march cut his way through the marshes toward the city.

San Juan, as its people and their visitors know, is situated on a small island off the coast of Puerto Rico. At that time it was connected to the mainland only by a narrow wooden bridge. It was there, on the mainland side of the bridge, that the English army arrived, four thousand strong, on the morning of June 16. Once more the defenders numbered only a handful of determined men. There were about 250 soldiers, and no more than 150 inexperienced settlers. Worse still, the Castle's batteries were turned toward the sea, and therefore were useless against a land attack. All Cumberland and his men had to do was to cross the bridge into the city. The brave Puerto Ricans barred their way and died in their tracks, all the way from the bridge through the passages to the fortress. But overwhelming numbers of English troops made Cumberland's victory inevitable.

Yet the unseen troubles which had haunted Drake and caused so many other expeditions to end in failure now made the English triumph at San Juan a very dangerous illusion. A mysterious plague was raging in the city, and once more the English dropped as though they had been mowed down by cannon. Houses and streets were choked with their bodies. Meanwhile, a Spanish resistance movement was taking shape. A Spanish officer, Captain Pedro Suárez, who had escaped from the Morro Castle, organized guerrilla bands and began to harass the English. The farmers refused to sell food to the invaders, and rather than give up their crops, they went about destroying their storehouse provisions.

All these troubles soon proved too much for the Eng-

lish. On November 23, the survivors left the island, and
on the same day, Captain Suárez entered San Juan
with his ragged guerrilla army. Cumberland had looted
the island of everything he could carry, but it was not
enough to appease Queen Elizabeth, who was highly
annoyed by this second failure.

Once more the Spanish flag flew over San Juan. Puerto
Rico had been under English rule for less than six
months. When news of the invasion reached the Spanish
King, he was alarmed enough to send an army of
3000 men as a reinforcement for the island. But by
the time they arrived in January 1599, the English
had long since gone. Only 400 of the arriving Spanish
soldiers remained; the others were sent back to Spain.
A new governor, who had arrived with the army, reported to the King that with the help of "the brave
sons of this country," he had more than enough man-
power to discourage any invader.

By the end of the 1500s, Puerto Ricans had shown
the world that they meant to survive on their island,
no matter what happened. They had survived every
kind of trouble and had fought for their land with
great courage. Those who lived through these times,
who had known what it was to endure hardship,
poverty, and war, were proud of their land. They were
willing to die, if necessary, to defend it.

The colony might have failed under the weight of
its troubles, but the settlers now were beginning to think
of themselves as the inhabitants of a country—in brief,
as Puerto Ricans.

Chapter 4

"Viva Puerto Rico!"

As the seventeenth century began, the island was still far from well off. Besides the capital city of San Juan there were only three other communities large enough to be called towns: San Blas (now Coamo), San Germán, and Arecibo. Of the four, San Juan was the largest. It had two hundred houses built of wood and stone, and a hundred *bohíos,* the Puerto Rican equivalent of a log cabin. There was also a cathedral which had no bells (the English had taken them as loot), two hospitals, and a small school.

This sounded like real progress. But grass grew in the streets, and the houses were more like isolated farm homes than town houses. Arecibo was typical of the smaller towns. Eighty families lived there, thirty of them Indians who had no quarrel with their neighbors. The citizens had pig farms and herds of cattle, but they had to go turtle fishing to get enough to live on.

Independent farmers lived on the remainder of the island. A few of them were successful, with large holdings of land, slaves, and paid workers. Most farmers, however, owned only small plots of land, and grew on it only enough to live. These people lived more and more in the mountains, and were later known as *jíbaros.*

For all their hard work and brave determination, the Puerto Rican settlers found their problems growing because of matters they could not control, and probably barely understood. Spain, for example, was in a state of decline, after being for a long time the most powerful

country in Europe. It was suffering from colonial indiges-
tion. Its economy was unable to absorb all the goods
produced in its far-flung Empire. Because of this, it
was necessary to limit the amount of goods the colonies
could sell to Spain. At the same time, ships carrying
goods from the mother country to its colonies were constantly under attacks by pirates. Merchant ships had to
be protected by warships, in convoys. This made the
transportation of goods so expensive that it added
sharply to the prices of the products being carried. Nor
could the colonists turn anywhere else. Spain had complete control of trade and would not permit the colonists
either to buy or sell in the amounts they required.

For the colonists there was one other solution, illegal
and risky. That was smuggling, and it soon appeared
there were French, English, Dutch and Portuguese
smugglers ready to take the risks and meet the demand.
The illegal sale of slaves also became an important
part of the smuggling trade, and soon was its most
profitable activity. It was impossible to prevent smuggling over so wide an area. Even if it had been, the
Crown's representatives whose job it was to stop smuggling were so badly paid they were easily bribed.

From an economic standpoint, Puerto Rico was worse
off than the other Spanish colonies. It was not a large
market for goods, so the Spanish merchant fleets usually
passed by. "It has been eleven years since we last saw
a ship," one governor complained. But the need for
clothing, medicines, metal tools, and other goods was
even greater in Puerto Rico than other colonies because
raw materials were so scarce. The settlers really had no
choice in the end. They could go on living under very
bad conditions, or they could go into smuggling on

a large scale. It was not surprising, then, that the forbidden trade was not only greater there than in the other colonies, but before long it had become the national sport.

Non-Spanish ships were trading openly everywhere along the island's coast. By the end of the 1600s, these illegal sales were so widespread that a special royal official was sent from Spain to investigate. What he found must have shocked him. Nearly everybody on the island was involved in the smuggling trade, from priests to soldiers, from town officials to farmers. The governor himself owned two ships engaged in the trade, and even ran a store in San Juan where the smuggled goods were sold.

The King's investigator was understandably unpopular. He was stopping, or threatening to stop, "business as usual," and possibly deny to citizens the trade that was keeping them alive. Feeling against him ran so high that he had to hide in a monastery to save his life.

Very few people were even punished. Smuggling continued to grow and it made life for most of the people of the island a little better. Conditions began to improve for the growing population. Most important, a new industry started which was to replace smuggling as the main source of income: coffee. Coffee bushes were brought to the island in 1755, and Puerto Rican coffee was soon known as the best in the world.

Even though smuggling had helped to keep the island's economy alive, it somehow never brought in the large number of African slaves which provided cheap forced labor for the big sugar plantations on the other West Indian islands and thus made these other colonies much richer. Only small quantities of sugar were produced in Puerto Rico, so large numbers of laborers were unnecessary. Crops that required little care were grown—products like ginger, for example, or those which could be produced with profit on small farms, like coffee. Slaves played only a small part in raising these crops. Some were smuggled in, but slavery never became really important to the Puerto Rican economy, and the citizens themselves, for the most part, disliked the whole idea of slavery. In later years, they argued with Spain to have it abolished entirely, and finally won the argument.

All these factors helped to make the island's population different from the others in the West Indies. In countries where sugar was the main crop, African slaves provided most of the labor on the plantations. Under this system, the Negro population came to far outnumber the white plantation owners, while slaves outnumbered the free Negroes. By contrast, in Puerto Rico at the end of the 1700s five out of every ten inhabitants were white, three were of mixed blood, one was a free Negro, and one a Negro slave.

These different groups had very good relations with each other and as a result Puerto Rico became a place of safety for runaway slaves from the English sugar islands of the Caribbean. The Spanish government declared that any slave arriving on the island would automatically be set free, because "it did not seem honorable for the king of Spain to enslave those who were asking for his protection." The newly freed slaves were given land and building materials in a section south of San Juan called Cangrejos (now Santurce), where they formed a hard-working community. Like other settlers, they organized a local militia which would help defend the capital if required.

Free Negroes were able to rise in the island's society, and sometimes the rise was spectacular. There was the story of Miguel Henríquez. Originally a shoemaker by trade, Henríquez so distinguished himself in the capture of pirate ships that the King gave him a captain's commission and a decoration known as the Royal Effigy, which carried with it the title of "gentleman." Eventually, Henríquez owned a fleet of ships. With these he often undertook royal assignments, including the capture from the English of the island of Vieques, off the coast of Puerto Rico.

In some ways, it seemed as though Puerto Ricans had gained because of their bad times. It was true, as one French observer noted, that "the possession of this island would have made the fortune of an active nation," but Spain had neglected it. This neglect had saved Puerto Rico from becoming a colony milked by Spain. Since there was no great wealth, those who lived there felt a greater sense of equality. Without a large slave population, racial tensions and class hatreds had little ground in which to grow. Visitors found the island not only "all green and beautiful," as it had always been, but the inhabitants possessed of "such natural kindness as to have no parallel in the rest of America." That was the finding of Marshall O'Reilly, who was sent by the King of Spain in 1765 to look into conditions in the island.

Another traveler agreed with this judgment. He was André Pierre Ledru, a young Frenchman who had been sent by his government on a scientific expedition and toured the island for eight months in 1797. Ledru stayed first in Loíza, at the house of Don Benito, a successful landowner. The "eternal greenery" of the island fasci-

nated Ledru as he wrote in his diary of how he break-
fasted on coconut milk and coffee "under the cool, fresh
shadow of green arches." Sometimes he lost his way
walking through the forest because he was so taken up
in admiring "the thousand pictures offered by nature."

Don Benito gave a party for his guest, to which he
invited about fifty friends. At this affair Ledru tasted
the fruits of the region—guavas, oranges, apricots, pa-
payas—and ate roast pig, the favorite food of Puerto
Ricans. He noted in his diary: "The Puerto Ricans love
dancing, and they never get tired of it." Everything
about the country pleased Ledru, especially Don Benito's
beautiful black-eyed daughter, Francisca. When he had
to leave at last for San Juan, he wrote with a lover's
sadness, "My heart remained with Francisca in Loíza."

In San Juan, he found it hard to be too sad about
Francisca. There was the same friendliness and hospi-
tality, and his hosts kept him busy with a round of
parties. He had an opportunity to see the horse races,
always staged during holiday celebrations, with compe-
titions among the best riders for a prize. Ledru thought
that all those in the races were excellent riders, including the girls, "who rode horses better than Pari-
sians."

No wonder the young Frenchman watched Puerto
Rico disappearing into the distance with such regret.
As his ship sailed out to sea, he wrote in his diary:
"What a difference between this island and the others
I have visited! Instead of cruelty, there is only kindness."

Not all visitors were so welcome. Invaders continued
to land on Puerto Rico's shores all through the 1600s
and 1700s. Sometimes they were nearly successful. In
1625, the commander of a Dutch fleet, Baudoin Henry,

managed to occupy San Juan by using much the same strategy that the English had employed, but with better luck. History was repeated. Morro Castle was placed under siege, while the male citizens joined the governor and the garrison in defending it, or else smuggled food into the fortress. Meanwhile, the mainland farmers organized guerrilla bands and harassed the invaders.

Henry threatened to burn the city unless the Morro surrendered. The governor answered: "You underestimate our courage. If you burn the city, the settlers have the strength to rebuild it. There is plenty of wood in the mountains. The people who are with me are more than enough to defeat you. Do what you want."

What Henry wanted to do was to burn San Juan, and he did, but in the end the governor proved himself correct. Under cover of darkness, he sent Captain Andrés Botello to take command of the guerrillas, instructing him to prepare to attack the city from the south. Inside the castle, the governor placed Captain Juan de Amézquita, a Puerto Rican, at the head of the soldiers and the Negro militia.

The signal was given. Botello and his guerrilla farmers advanced and fought their way into the city, while at the same time, crying "Viva Puerto Rico!" Amézquita and his soldiers fell upon the Dutch from the castle. Caught in this trap, the invaders fled as fast as they could to rescue boats sent from their fleet in the harbor.

Some of the fighting in the city was hand-to-hand, and there is a tradition that at one point Captain Amézquita found himself in combat with Henry and wounded the Dutch commander, who died soon after.

When the King heard about the heroism of the governor and the islanders, he sent them rewards of money and praised Puerto Rico by referring to it as "the vanguard of my West Indies."

He had continuing reason to be proud. In 1702, thirty settlers from the local militia of Arecibo, under Captain Antonio Correa, drove off another English attack, during which Correa himself killed the English captain. To this day Arecibo is known in folklore as the "villa of Captain Correa." There were similar struggles against invaders at Loíza and Guadianilla. The King sent money rewards to these places, again praising the courage of Puerto Ricans—"so few in number," he said, "but so well endowed with quality, that with them on my side I do not fear any mishaps."

His faith was not misplaced, as further events showed. In 1797, the Puerto Ricans displayed to the Crown, and to the world, their bravest moment. England and Spain were at war in that year, and an English fleet had been sent to the Caribbean. When the news reached Puerto Rico that nearby Trinidad had been taken by these new invaders, the whole country prepared for war.

While women were busy storing food and supplies for the expected siege, the local militia forces from Ponce, Añasco, Manatí, Utuado, and other towns gathered in San Juan. They were a wildly different lot. Those from Pepino were commanded by their priest. A young lieutenant from Toa Baja, named Pepe Díaz, led fifty men. The Andino brothers of San Juan headed a group of volunteers who intended to police the beaches. Rafael García brought sixty men in light boats (*piraguas*) from the Cangrejos militia to help prevent English landing boats from reaching the beaches.

Preparations were no more than completed when the English arrived. Their fleet approached Cangrejos on

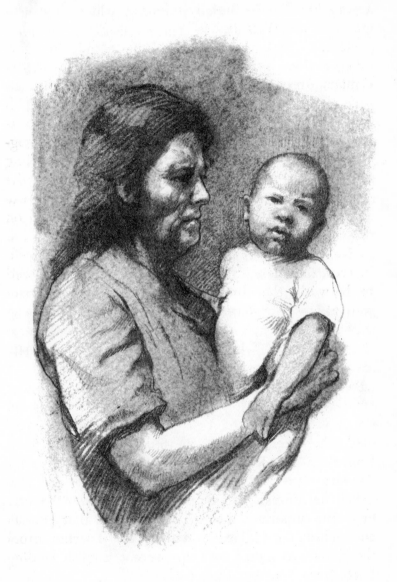

Puerto Rican families were a mixture of Indian, Spanish, and African blood.

April 18th and demanded surrender, which of course the governor refused to do. The English then prepared to land.

But the Puerto Ricans had learned something from earlier invasions. Now San Juan was protected by two more forts, San Gerónimo and San Cristóbal, as well as by several fortifications hastily built by the various militia bodies. Into this arc of defenses the British landed their forces and soon found themselves attacked from every side, while the Puerto Rican guns battered their ships. So fierce was the islanders' resistance that the invaders could not even establish a beachhead secure enough to hold. Frustrated and suffering heavy losses, the fleet left on May 2.

Next day a mass of thanks was offered at the cathedral. The bishop blessed the men, and after the mass, the militia troops disbanded and went back to their towns. With them they took the memory of a hero—Pepe Díaz, who had been killed at the bridge of Martín Peña. His name became a symbol of the defense of 1797, and when they sang of him in a popular folksong, the voice of a new national spirit could be heard:

> Pepe Díaz was the bravest man
> The King of Spain ever had.

Pepe Díaz was a national hero, but he was more than that. The important thing about him was that he was not Spanish, nor Indian, nor African, but "Puerto Rican."

Chapter 5

When Pepe Díaz died in 1797, the man who would become the first Puerto Rican leader was already twenty-two and an officer in the Spanish Navy. His name was Ramón Power, born in San Juan in 1775, the son of a navy man.

With such a tradition, it was natural that Ramón and his brother José should want to become career officers. But it was not easy to get the necessary schooling in a country where the lack of education had left 70 per cent of the population unable to read. There were a few elementary schools, and only two high schools, run by the Dominican and Franciscan priests in San Juan. Advanced studies could be taken in philosophy and theology, at the Dominican House. The children of the rich were taught at home by private tutors, then had to be sent back to Europe to finish their studies. Fortunately, the Power children were in this class. By the time Ramón was twelve, he and his brother had learned all that their tutor could teach them. They were then sent to Spain and France to complete their education.

At the time they left there was an air of hope in the island. There were now 34 towns, and the population had jumped to 150,000. The restriction on trade was gradually being removed, and that had been the major complaint of the Puerto Ricans. While Spain fought various wars with England and France, after 1778, the King issued decrees permitting trade with neutral nations. This relaxing of restrictions could not have come at a better time.

Since the 1700s, the French colony of Haiti had been the chief source of tropical products for the world market. Beginning in 1791, however, a series of slave revolts led to fierce and bloody fighting on Haiti. It ended with the independence of the colony in 1804. But the killing and destruction had been so great during the struggle that Haiti could no longer supply its tropical products for export. Other Caribbean colonies, including Puerto Rico, quickly took advantage of the situation.

The United States, newly independent itself, and without colonies of its own, was especially interested in developing sources of trade. Puerto Rico and Cuba were the nearest, most obvious sources of supply. Thus began the long economic association of these countries with their northern neighbor. So fast did trade grow that Puerto Ricans realized their commerce with the United States would be greater than that with Spain. It might even replace it if the Spanish government continued to follow its relaxed trading policy.

Spain, however, was in the middle of another of its arguments about the proper role of a king, and how an imperial power should deal with its colonies. The Power brothers discovered this when they reached Madrid. Ramón thought much about the questions being raised, but meanwhile he had another job to do. He went on to France and learned the French language. In that country he found the citizens ready to accept a strong man's rule, if he could only restore peace and order after the chaos of the French Revolution. The strong man who appeared was Napoleon. The historic actions he was about to take would, among other things, radically change the history of both Spain and Latin America.

Ramón returned home a lieutenant in the Navy. He found his countrymen arguing about the revolutions which were sweeping the world, and the advantages and disadvantages of Spanish rule.

Power thought a great deal about the problems of his island and what might be done about them. As he left the island again to continue his navy service, he promised himself that if the day came when Puerto Rico needed a man like himself who was familiar with the questions of the day as he was, he would do his best to help. Meanwhile, in 1802, he was given command of his first ship.

Sweeping through Europe on the path of conquest, Napoleon had brought most of the Continent under control by 1808. Moving into Spain, he forced the King to renounce his crown. He then compelled Ferdinand, the King's son and heir, into exile and prison. Napoleon then sent his own brother to be king, which made Spain little better than a colony of France. Angry and rebellious, the Spaniards set up a provisional government in the name of Ferdinand. In Puerto Rico, the citizens followed the example of the rest of Spanish America and declared themselves loyal to King Ferdinand.

Seeking to help the Crown in a more solid way, the islanders decided to attack the French colony of Santo Domingo. By this time Ramón Power was home again with units of the Spanish Navy. Under his command, these ships joined an English fleet and sailed off to conquer Santo Domingo. The conquest was surprisingly easy. Overnight, Power became a hero to his countrymen, because he had directed the decisive battle of the campaign and the French had surrendered to him.

Power soon had another opportunity to serve his country. The Spanish provisional government declared the colonies "an integral part of the Spanish monarchy." This meant that the colonies would be represented when the Cortes, the Spanish legislature, met at Cádiz, the provisional capital in southern Spain. There was no doubt in the minds of most Puerto Ricans about whom their representative should be. They chose Ramón Power. On September 24, 1810, the first deputy from Puerto Rico took his seat in the Cortes. Power then cast his lot with those who wanted to give Spain a modern constitution. His speeches were so eloquent and convincing, and he became so popular as the spokesman for the colonies, that the Spanish Cortes elected him its vice-president —a great honor indeed. It was the highest post a Puerto Rican would ever hold in the Spanish government. Immediately, Power proposed a bill limiting the authority of the governor of Puerto Rico, so that he would only be concerned with the defense of the island, while a civilian official, an "intendant," would be in charge of all non-military matters. The Power bill passed, and the Cortes asked Ramón to choose the new intendant. He named an economist, Alejandro Ramírez, instructing him to promote the economic development of the island.

Puerto Rico welcomed Ramírez with enthusiasm. In a year he worked such wonders that tax collections more than tripled, reflecting the island's sudden increase in wealth. Later the Puerto Ricans said of him: "He found us wearing rags, but when he left, we were wearing silk!"

The Cortes went ahead meantime with more reform

legislation. In 1812, it produced the first Spanish Constitution, by which Puerto Rico, with the other colonies,
became a province of Spain. Its people were now
Spanish citizens. Local affairs were to be controlled by
a local legislature, and they were to be represented in
the Cortes.

A burst of joy swept the island when the news of
the Constitution came. There was music in the streets.
Public and private dances were held everywhere. Horse
races, fireworks, and banquets competed with each other
for attention. Churches held solemn high masses of
thanks. In the midst of it came the sorrowful news:
Ramón Power was dead in Spain, a victim of yellow
fever.

It was 1813 and Puerto Rico had come a long way
since that day in 1775 when Power was born. A great
deal had been gained in his lifetime, but sadly, most
of it was soon to be lost. The islanders mourned their
dead leader, consoled by the new freedom of the Constitution.

But a fresh time of troubles began. Napoleon was
defeated at last in 1814, and King Ferdinand returned
to the Spanish throne from captivity. Almost his first
act was to do away with the Constitution. This had a
revolutionary effect in Latin America. The colonies,
which had become provinces under the Constitution,
were now colonies again. Renewed fighting broke out
in many places, and a determined effort began to drive
Spain out of the New World. In Puerto Rico there was a
more cautious feeling of "wait and see."

As the struggle went on in Spain between the King
and the Constitutionalists, Ferdinand eventually had to
give in before the threat of popular revolution. As a

result of the continuing confusion, however, his colonial empire fell apart until the only Spanish colonies that remained in the Western Hemisphere were Puerto Rico and Cuba.

Even after most of the colonies were lost, political unrest continued in Spain. The Constitution was the major issue. Since constitutional changes in Spain affected the island, Puerto Ricans hardly knew from one day to the next what their status might be. One day they might hear they were a province, and then the next ship would bring news that the Constitution had been done away with and that they had become a colony again.

Governors came and went. Most of them were suspicious, domineering men who meant to keep Puerto Rico loyal to Spain no matter what happened. They refused to believe that Puerto Ricans showed little willingness to be anything but loyal. The islanders had looked around at the newly formed independent governments in the former Spanish Empire. Here revolution followed revolution and governments appeared and disappeared, which made Puerto Ricans fearful of independence. The island was a place where peace and order prevailed much more than in the ex-colonies. Puerto Ricans wanted to keep things that way.

As it happened, most of the governors took a real interest in the island's problems. While they suppressed anything that looked to them like an independence movement, they also improved schools, built roads and hospitals, and promoted economic welfare. Therefore, conditions were not so bad that people would turn their thoughts to revolution. Nevertheless, there was much that bothered the islanders.

First of all, everything had to be done in accordance with the governor's will. If a corrupt or cruel governor was appointed, the citizens could only appeal to Spain and wait for an answer. In the end, the official was recalled, but it took a very long time. Even under the best of governors, there was no such thing as due process of law.

People could not forget the story of General Prim and "The Eagle." When the general arrived in Puerto Rico in December 1847 to be governor, he had found in the city jail a horse thief popularly known as "The Eagle," who had become famous in the island for his activities around the town of Cabo Rojo. He would steal from under anybody's nose, and if he was caught, he had no trouble escaping. This time he had been sent to San Juan and kept under the tightest possible security. But the general liked The Eagle's cockiness, and promised to let him go if he would behave and stay within the city limits of San Juan. The Eagle promised. "If you trick me," the general warned him, "I will have you shot." A few months later, Prim decided to tour the island, arriving one day in Cabo Rojo. That very evening his favorite horse was stolen from the stable, even though the place was lighted and under guard. It could only have been The Eagle, and so it was. He returned the horse next day, saying he wanted to show the general how good he was at his trade. Prim didn't see the joke. All he knew was that the thief had broken his promise to stay in San Juan. The Eagle was shot without trial next day.

This incident sent a wave of dismay among the people. Everybody knew The Eagle was a convicted thief, but he had been given only jail terms for all his previous

"The Eagle" would steal from under anybody's nose, and if he was caught, he had no trouble escaping.

thefts, and this time he had not really committed an offense, it was said, because he had returned the horse. It was clear that he had been shot only because he had broken a promise to the governor.

Appeals were made to the court in charge of Puerto Rican affairs, protesting the governor's action. General Prim defended himself on the ground that his word was law in the island, which no one had any reason to doubt. Nevertheless, he had obviously created so much ill will that the Crown thought it best to recall him, although he was never punished for his action. The Eagle's death made it plainer than ever that any governor could do whatever he liked in Puerto Rico, and it was possible to do a great deal of harm before an appeal to Spain could help matters.

No doubt there would have been more unrest if the island's economic situation had not improved so much. Agricultural production had increased, especially sugar, which had become a highly profitable crop even though it had to follow the ups and downs of the American market. This was a mixed blessing, however. Now that large sugar plantations were no longer rare in Puerto Rico, a real difference was being introduced between rich and poor. Until then, the richest and the poorest had not been separated by a wide gap and Puerto Ricans had gone through good and bad times together. Sugar changed this. More and more *jíbaros* were finding it impossible to survive on their small patches of land, and had to hire themselves out for very little money. It was forbidden to import slaves, but the mere fact that slavery still existed brought down the price of free labor even more.

Rather than work long hours in the field for a miserable wage, many *jíbaros* fell into a state of complete idleness. They stood around and did nothing. Half-starved and diseased, they were beginning to be a serious problem. To some of the governors, their behavior was simple laziness. A series of decrees were sent out saying that those who did not have a job or did not own property were considered vagrants, to be dealt with by the authorities. Such decrees only made the problem worse. Puerto Rican demands for more effective programs got nowhere.

The final and major complaint of Puerto Ricans was the refusal of Spain to do away with slavery. Petitions were being continuously sent to Madrid asking for a law that would abolish slavery and guarantee citizenship rights to free Negroes. These petitions caused a sensation in Europe. Here were colonials, slaveholders themselves, who were demanding to free their slaves legally, no matter what the cost.

Waiting for the Spanish government to act could take forever. Therefore, Puerto Ricans formed an Association for the Abolition of Slavery. Membership in the Association grew and money contributions came from all over the island. The members hit upon a clever scheme to get around slavery laws. As slave babies were brought to be baptized, they would be bought by the Association and then set free. The scheme not only kept the number of slaves down but also allowed these babies to grow up as free men. At the same time, the Association helped and protected the many adult slaves who would be set free by their masters.

Most everyone in the island, therefore, agreed that something had to be done about the arbitrary rule of the governor, about the increasing poverty of the work-

ers, and about the inhuman institution of slavery. Most
of the workers—the great majority of the population,
for that matter—could not read and found it hard to
express their complaints in any way. They had no position, no influence, no bargaining power. They were
afraid of the authorities, the police, their employers,
everyone—and with reason.

The only people able to protest were the richer,
better educated classes, but they too were hemmed in
at every turn. One of the worst governors, General
Pezuela, was so eager to restrict freedom of association
that no one could give a party in his home without
official permission. Once he jailed two rich merchants,
without trial, and eventually deported them, simply because they had attended a meeting of businessmen
which had not been officially approved.

It was the educated and wealthy who had been
among the founders of the Association for the Abolition
of Slavery. They were men like Ramón Betances, from
Cabo Rojo, who had a medical degree from the University of Paris, and Segundo Ruiz Belvis, of San Germán, who had a law degree from the University of
Madrid. Soon Betances, Ruiz Belvis, and their friends
found themselves in trouble with the authorities.

By the middle of the nineteenth century, the island
was in a state of tension. Some became convinced that
the only solution was independence. Since this meant
complete separation from Spain, they were known as
"separatists." Betances was among them. However, independence still did not appeal to the majority of
Puerto Ricans for complete separation from Spain could
only be secured with a bloody revolution. It was a long
time now—since the days of the Indians and the Con-

When the governor discovered plans for a revolt, he had some of the rebels executed.

quistadores—that the island had seen the horrors of civil war. As a rule, those men who were active in Puerto Rican politics did not approve of violence. Instead, they really believed that "liberties can be secured without bloodshed."

That there was little support for revolutionary action was proven in 1868. Inspired by Betances, who was then in exile, independence sympathizers had been meeting in secrecy. Leadership groups, known as *juntas,* had been formed and a plan for revolution agreed upon. The conspiracy was betrayed before the preparations had been completed. Nevertheless, a few *junta* leaders marched on September 23 into the small town of Lares, and amid cries of "Long live Puerto Rico!" proclaimed the island an independent republic. They had about 300 men for an army, mostly their own workers whom they had pressed into service, with no military experience and with machetes for weapons. The proclamation failed to get any support from the population, and it was hardly surprising that this force was defeated in less than a week by the governor's soldiers.

It was now clear that patience and persistence were as much a part of the Puerto Rican personality as the will to survive. In spite of the disappointments of Spanish rule, Puerto Ricans were united in the belief that evolution, no matter how slow, was better than revolution. For the rest of the century, this belief was to create for the island a tradition of non-violent political action. When the United States became the ruling power after Spain, the non-violent tradition had been well established.

Chapter 6

Political Dogfights

With revolution out of the question, the separatists remained outside the mainstream of Puerto Rican politics. Since they could not operate legally, most went into exile. They settled mainly in New York where their activities were of little use in influencing events in the island. The field was left to two other groups, known as liberals and conservatives.

The liberals were divided among themselves. Some would insist that Puerto Rico should try to regain the status of a Spanish province. Since they were for "assimilation," with Spain, they were called *asimilistas*. The present statehood parties in Puerto Rico are like the *asimilistas* in that they want the island to become a state of the United States.

Other liberals were in favor of some form of self-rule, or autonomy. As they explained it, autonomy would permit the island to control its own affairs while remaining associated with Spain. Under self-rule, the power of the governor would be lessened but the island would still receive the military protection of Spanish authority. The present day Commonwealth of Puerto Rico—or Free Associated State—is a special type of autonomy.

Among the liberals was Ramón Baldorioty de Castro, who time after time, was elected as deputy to the Cortes from Puerto Rico. This man, who would one day be the liberals' most important leader, was the illegitimate son of a Spaniard and a Puerto Rican woman.

His intelligence and hard work as a student had won him scholarships to study in France and Spain. But like so many other Puerto Ricans before and after, he wanted to use what he had learned in service to his island. Baldorioty favored a republican form of government in Spain, and some kind of autonomy or "commonwealth" status for Puerto Rico.

What all liberals wanted most for the island was to have it stop being a mere colony. Only then, they believed, would it solve its economic problems. The conservatives, on the other hand, thought the question of status should not be pressed one way or the other. In principle they were willing to accept whatever political relationship Spain might order, because they considered themselves "loyal subjects." The liberals understood what that meant. It made them "disloyal subjects," of course.

As far as the conservatives were concerned, Puerto Rico did not have to wait to solve its economic problems until its status was finally determined. In fact, they had an advanced program to improve the economic conditions of the island, a program which also had the backing of the liberals. The two groups really differed only on political questions, but it was a big difference.

When they formed themselves into political parties, the conservatives became known as *incondicionales*, meaning that they were for Spain without any conditions, as opposed to the liberals. Then followed a long period of maneuvering between the two Puerto Rican factions, the *liberales* and the *incondicionales*. The game they began to play during this period continued to have a bad effect on political life in Puerto Rico for a long time. In order to win, each side would try to get the support of the governor. The party which failed to win him over would then try to use whatever influence it possessed in Madrid to have him recalled. Both parties, then, came to depend more and more on the shifting course of political events in Spain, and the support each could obtain there. The *incondicionales* usually won the game, but at least the Puerto Rican liberals had the satisfaction of knowing that there were many in Spain who shared their ideas and aims, and were having just as hard a time trying to make them into reality.

An important turn of events in Spain finally came in February 1873. The King handed his resignation to the Cortes and left the country. The Cortes then met in full and declared Spain a republic. After such a fundamental step was taken, enthusiasm for reform was overwhelming. The Puerto Rican deputies realized that this was the time to bring up again their demands for abolition of slavery. They were right. On March 22, 1873, during the final session, the Cortes responded by passing a law doing away with slavery "forever on the island of Puerto Rico."

When this news came by cable to San Juan, there was an outburst of public joy. People paraded in the streets, and went to the churches to hold ceremonies of public thanks. The news raced by word of mouth from town to town, and from farm to farm. Cries of "Viva!" heralded its passage. Soon the whole island was celebrating. No protests were heard; everyone seemed to be congratulating the freed slaves.

The victory of the Puerto Rican deputies, who had been able to persuade the Cortes to grant one of the island's major demands, gave the *liberales* hope that

The whole island celebrated the end of slavery, and people crowded the churches to give thanks.

a change in the colonial status was near. The island deputies could be expected to maintain the excellent reputation they had built in the Cortes. And the people of Puerto Rico had matched the record of its deputies by their humanitarian behavior concerning the institution of slavery, a behavior which had impressed both Spanish and foreign observers. The new Republican Government in Spain seemed favorably inclined. "If only because of its culture," said the preamble to the government's election decree, "the island of Puerto Rico deserves to enjoy all the liberties that other civilized peoples enjoy."

Unfortunately, as had happened so often before, Puerto Ricans were to see their hopes disappointed. They would have to wait another twenty-five years for autonomy. The Republican Government did not last long. The Constitution which the newly elected Cortes proposed was too much of a break with the past. Old line army officers moved into the argument, and early in 1874 forced the Republican Cortes to dissolve. Then came a reaction to the Republic's progressive ideas. The Army ran the government in Spain, and in Puerto Rico destroyed nearly everything the liberals had been able to get done. The repressive army generals went too far at home, however, and late in 1874 a new junta, a more moderate one, took power and proclaimed a limited monarchy, with young Prince Alfonso on the throne.

In the constitutional changes that followed, the status of Puerto Rico remained as before. The island could continue to have representation in the Spanish Cortes, but it was not legally a province. Furthermore, the new Constitution was phrased in such a way that it implied the island could never become a province. As a result, the *asimilistas* among the liberals found themselves without a cause.

Baldorioty, who had always been for autonomy, moved into the front line to reorganize the liberals. He succeeded in founding a new Autonomist Party, which united the different factions among the liberals behind the idea of self-rule. The party approved a platform that became a model for future political action, and planned for the island almost the same form of government it has today. This platform, the result of many compromises, was known as the Ponce Plan. It was signed not only by men of Baldorioty's age, but by younger men like Luis Muñoz Rivera and José Celso Barbosa, who would soon become important in Puerto Rican affairs.

But life was hard for the Autonomists. If one managed to get elected, the *incondicionales* took the election to court. In the courts the decision would be nearly always in favor of the Autonomists. The decision might not be of much use, however. Muñoz Rivera, for example, after being elected to the local legislature, had to go through so many appeals that when he was finally entitled to his seat legally, his term was over. As for journalists, it became an occupational hazard for them to be arrested and released.

The Autonomists could not help but be discouraged. They began to fight among themselves, each blaming the other for the party's troubles. Moderates were accused of trying to make deals with the *incondicionales*. The militants were charged with making things worse for the party. Nearly everyone was accused of trying to control the party for his own purposes, which was a sad joke, because by then there was really no party to control. Baldorioty had kept all the factions more or less united. But he died in 1889 and the other older leaders were too taken up with the past to be able to lead the younger men toward a reasonable future. Discouraged, some of these leaders retired to private life.

It seemed as if Puerto Rico was becoming a sleepy tropical colony where the intellectuals talked to each other in an elegant language no one else could understand, while the masses had nothing left but to work and hope.

Chapter 7

Autonomy at Last

By the 1890s, educational facilities were greatly improved. Art and letters were flourishing. There were men like Eugenio María de Hostos whose brilliant essays on politics, philosophy, and literature form part of the intellectual history of Latin America. Poets like José Gautier Benítez and Alejandro Tapia made the nineteenth century the "golden century" of Puerto Rican literature. Painters like Francisco Oller, whose works may be seen in European museums, carried on the artistic traditions of the island.

However, the political and economic situation had not changed. To stir itself out of stagnation, Puerto Rico needed new blood, and the rising generation provided it in the persons of three men: Luis Muñoz Rivera, José Celso Barbosa, and José de Diego, each one of them representing a different viewpoint.

Of the three, Muñoz Rivera was probably the most practical. He grew impatient with endless arguments about the fine points of politics. He felt that the brilliant articles and pamphlets constantly being written by some of the Autonomists were a waste of time. As far as Muñoz was concerned, it was the results which were important, and as far as he could see, the Autonomists were getting nowhere.

Muñoz believed that autonomy had to be gained quickly or else conditions on the island would get out of control. If the *incondicionales* were able to rule by making a puppet out of the governor, the Autonomists would have to find some other method, he reasoned. One suggested itself to him. If one could only anticipate which political party was about to come to power in Spain, a deal could be made with that party before it took over the government.

What, Muñoz asked himself, could the Autonomists promise such a Spanish party? For one thing, to keep the island Spanish and make it a model of good government. This could only reflect to the credit of Spain in the eyes of the rest of the world, where Madrid's image was badly tarnished. In exchange, Puerto Rico could be granted autonomy, with the Autonomist Party in charge of making it work.

This clever idea, Muñoz believed, would be a way of going over the heads of both the *incondicionales* and the governor. With the backing of the Spanish party in power, before it got there, the Autonomists could break the hold of their rivals. And Muñoz had a definite idea which party might next be in power. It would be the party led by Sagasta, a liberal monarchist.

Muñoz's idea was not shared by José Barbosa, the second of the three young men. Barbosa, a Negro doctor, was the son of poor parents, and had risen to a high place in the medical profession through hard work. A graduate of the University of Michigan, he had lived in the States and had come to know its political life and admired it, to the point of being a confirmed defender of republican government. He wanted the Autonomist Party to come to power by essentially the same route he had taken—through hard work, good organization, and democratic methods. Muñoz Rivera's idea of "political deals" repelled him, and even if he ever approved of such a thing, it would certainly not be a deal with Sagasta's monarchist party, no matter how liberal it was. The deal would have to be with one of the republican parties. Barbosa also pointed out the clear danger involved if Muñoz happened to back a loser. The Autonomist Party would be finished for good then. In any case, said Barbosa, he would not trust the promises of a monarchist.

The third man of this trio was José de Diego, a lawyer by profession and a poet by inclination. As a student in Spain, his poems had attracted some attention but he had left behind all thoughts of a literary career and now was devoting his life to his island's interests. He wrote patriotic poems, and his single dream was independence. He thought autonomy only a second-best arrangement, but if Muñoz had some way to get it, he would take his side and help. His help was not inconsiderable. De Diego was a charming man and a wonderful speaker, who would have been a help to any politician.

In spite of the somewhat different viewpoints they held, most of the Autonomists fell in behind these three men, and for a while there was some degree of cooperation among them. In 1894, Barbosa took charge of reorganizing the party and began rebuilding it from the grassroots. He traveled from town to town, making speeches, distributing literature, and strengthening the local committees. In his first year the results were impressive. Enthusiasm was rising again. Most of it, however, was not in support of Muñoz Rivera's plan. Even those who accepted the idea in principle wondered how it would be put into action. They were not nearly as certain as Muñoz which party it would be best to back.

With or without support, Muñoz decided to act on

his own. He sailed for Spain in April 1896, and in Madrid headed straight for the cafés, always the centers of political talk. He made friends, listened, and talked, and met Spanish politicians. In Puerto Rico he had not really cared which Spanish party he would back as long as it was a winner, and it had seemed to him that the Spanish republicans would not win again. In Spain, he found his judgment was right.

Returning to Puerto Rico in January 1896, he was willing to admit that the republicans were the "standard bearers of a beautiful vision," and expressed himself in sympathy with their ideals. Yet it was only a vision, he declared. "In Spain the only honorable thing to do would be to join them," he said, "but it is absurd for us Puerto Ricans to forget our interests in pursuit of a dream." On the other hand, he reported, he had talked to Sagasta and his men and found them favorable to the idea of autonomy. Moreover, they did not like the *incondicionales.* "They are causing more troubles than the hairs I have in my head!" Sagasta had complained.

At a meeting of Autonomist Party leaders in June 1896, Muñoz made a complete report on his journey and strongly presented his case. "As of now," he said, "we are nothing; we accomplish nothing. The vitality of Puerto Rico is being destroyed. The colonial government is wealthy, but poverty among the population increases. When are we going to act?"

There could be no question about the poverty. Every person who studied the situation of the poor was shocked by what he found. Salvador Brau, one of the few who had examined the condition of the working class, wrote a report which was a harsh indictment of the colonial regime. Speaking of the *jíbaros,* another observer, Dr. Coll y Toste, remarked: "The man who harvests the best coffee in the world cannot afford to drink it, and when he can get a cup of coffee, he has to sweeten it with molasses because sugar is too expensive."

Muñoz had all this in his mind when he challenged the party leaders at the June 1896 meeting: "How can we benefit the population unless we move?" While everyone did not share his views completely, a compromise was reached at the meeting. They agreed to choose a commission of five men to go to Spain, to talk with the leaders of the several political parties, and work out an alliance. As was fitting, Muñoz was one of the five.

The commission arrived in Spain in September 1896. They began at once talking to the leaders, whose reactions were mixed. One of the republican leaders admitted that hopes of achieving a republic in Spain were indeed remote. Others refused to say anything. Sagasta, however, was quite ready to try and work out an alliance, and Muñoz did so, with the support of two other members of the commission. Eventually an agreement with the monarchists was written down and agreed upon, and the document was ready to be taken back and approved by a full meeting of the Autonomist Party.

On February 11, 1897, Muñoz came home to San Juan. It was seven o'clock in the morning when he arrived, but half the town was there to receive him. He spent the rest of that day talking with the Autonomists, trying to get support for the meeting that was to take place the following day. Circumstances were working for him. A new revolution had flared up in Cuba in

1895, and those Puerto Ricans working for independence from New York and Paris with the Cuban revolutionaries were attracting a great deal of attention.

Muñoz sympathized with them. He had even told Sagasta during the negotiations that if his proposals were not accepted he intended to join the New York group. But the pact he now proposed to offer the Autonomist meeting offered the practical results of independence without the need for a bloody revolution. When he outlined the plan next day, the party members grasped this idea at once and approved the pact.

Only Barbosa remained against it. After the assembly's approving vote was announced, he left the meeting, accompanied by those who still favored an understanding with the Spanish republicans.

The remaining delegates then turned their attention to founding a new party. It would be called the Liberal Party, and Muñoz was elected its president. Barbosa and his followers decided to start their own party, calling it the Pure Autonomist Party, with Manuel Fernández Juncos as president. Later the two groups reorganized and changed their names several times, but they were always unofficially called *muñocistas* and *barbosistas* after their founders.

Less than a month after the birth of the new Liberal Party, the headlines in Puerto Rican newspapers bore out Muñoz' good judgment: SAGASTA COMES TO POWER! Thus the first prediction had come true. Now it remained to be seen if Muñoz's further ideas were also correct, and Sagasta would grant autonomy to Puerto Rico. A few months later, Muñoz's own paper, *La Democracia*, confirmed that belief too: AUTONOMY A FACT! Sagasta had announced on the afternoon of November 9, 1897, that his cabinet had unanimously approved a charter of autonomy for the island. Muñoz Rivera was completely vindicated.

The charter set up a parliamentary system in Puerto Rico, much like those of European countries. The governor was to be called governor-general. Although he was to be the representative of the Spanish Crown his powers were limited. Real power lay in the hands of an elected Insular Parliament and the ministers of the parliamentary cabinet. No order from the governor, for example, could go into effect until it was countersigned by one of the elected ministers. Moreover, the Insular Parliament had the power to make commercial treaties with foreign countries. Treaties made by Spain, on the other hand, would not bind the island unless the island's Parliament gave approval.

At the same time, Puerto Rico was not to lose its representation in Spain; nineteen deputies were to be elected to the Spanish legislature.

Finally, the charter was irrevocable, meaning that it could not be suspended or changed without the approval both of the Spanish government and the Insular Parliament.

Sagasta wanted the charter to become effective as soon as possible, and he urged the two factions of Autonomists to reunite. Everyone was agreed that a temporary cabinet should be named, while waiting for elections for the Parliament. On February 10, 1898, Governor-General Macías appointed the new cabinet, composed of four *muñocistas*, three *barbosistas*, and no *incondicionales*. Muñoz held the most important post: he was Minister of Justice.

Within a week the cabinet was sworn in and the

Charter of Autonomy came into effect. There were wild mass demonstrations all over Puerto Rico in support of the charter. In San Juan, more than six thousand people staged a procession from Columbus Square, at one end of the city, to the governor-general's palace at the other end. Muñoz Rivera, de Diego, Barbosa, and Fernández Juncos were the major speakers, while Baldorioty looked down benevolently on them from pictures carried by the crowd.

At last, Puerto Rico had come into its own.

Chapter 8

Americans Take Over

Whatever the Charter of Autonomy might have been able to accomplish will never be known. A war between the United States and Spain, which Puerto Ricans did nothing to bring about, ended its life and created a wholly new situation.

Even as Puerto Ricans danced in the streets, cheering their good fortune that February day in 1898, the American battleship *Maine* was blown up and sunk in Havana Harbor. This gave American warhawks who were calling for battle the excuse they needed to go to war against Spain. While Puerto Ricans were going to the polls to elect their first Insular Parliament, sharp diplomatic exchanges were taking place between the United States and Spain. War was near.

Puerto Ricans hardly noticed the danger. They were too involved in the verbal war going on between the *muñocistas* and the *barbosistas* over the way the elections were run. The results had given twenty-five seats in Parliament to the Muñoz party, with five going to the Barbosa party and two split among other groups. This Liberal majority was probably the result of Muñoz Rivera's popularity, as his party claimed, but the *barbosistas* said it was at least partly the result of fraud in the elections. Neither side could prove it was right.

While the argument continued, on April 25, 1898, the United States declared war on Spain. This war was to affect the island far more than the Charter of Autonomy. Historians still argue its causes, but officially, its chief aim, as far as the United States was concerned, was to secure Cuba's independence from Spain.

A full-scale revolution had been raging in Cuba since 1895. It had left the Spanish government with only three choices: to give Cuba independence, to put down the revolution and return the island to its status as a colony, or to conciliate the revolutionaries by giving them the same kind of autonomy that had been given to Puerto Rico.

The blowing up of the *Maine* brought matters to a climax. It was widely believed in the United States that the Spaniards had blown up the ship. This was never proved, then or later, and it could well have been an accident. President William McKinley had sent the *Maine* down to Havana to "show the flag," and point out to Spain that the United States thought her interests were at stake. Those interests were largely American-owned plantations and businesses in Cuba which the revolution was destroying. Trade with Cuba had come to a standstill.

For their part, the Spaniards needed no reminder of American military power. In fact their policy in Cuba was based on the belief that other nations would stay out of the war. Spain was no longer a great power. She knew she might be able to beat the Cubans, but she could certainly not win against the United States. There was no reason, then, for her to sink the *Maine,* which could only make the Americans even angrier.

It was with some desperation, therefore, and in the hope of preventing the United States from becoming involved, that Spain offered an armistice to the Cuban rebels and a grant of autonomy. The time had passed for compromise, however. Scenting victory with the help of America, the rebels now said they wanted only independence. McKinley virtually guaranteed it when he asked Congress on April 11, 1898, for a declaration of war, asserting that intervention in Cuba was necessary.

"Imperialism" and "colonialism" were already sweeping European nations at the close of the 1800s. Now America was joining in. Theodore Roosevelt, who had just become Assistant Secretary of the Navy, expressed the most common mood of the American public when he wrote: "No triumph of peace is quite so great as the supreme triumphs of war." America's first venture into imperialism was an ideal one, since the Philippines and Cuba and Puerto Rico were all controlled only by the weak power of Spain. Even in the early days of the Republic, Thomas Jefferson had dreamed of the American flag flying over Cuba, and all through the 1800s the United States had at different times tried to buy both Cuba and Puerto Rico from Spain. Now war would do what money had been unable to accomplish.

By becoming involved in Cuba, everyone's interests would be satisfied. Business would be made safe. The islands would make good navy bases. From this somewhat easy conquest, the United States would emerge as a world power. Of course Cuba would have to be made independent, but that could be done in the form of an American protectorate. Nothing was said about the future of Puerto Rico and the Philippines, except for Theodore Roosevelt's demand that "there should not be any talk of peace" until those islands, too, were secured by the Americans. And that was how "the war to liberate Cuba" became also, in time, a way for the United States to annex Puerto Rico.

The first shot of the war in Puerto Rico was fired at

noon on May 10, 1898, at an American ship, the *Yale*. The islanders had been watching American ships prowling off the coasts for more than a month, but they were so far offshore that people had called them "ghosts," seen dimly through the sea mists. The *Yale* had come a little too close, however. She was not hit, but the incident was enough to put both sides on the alert.

Strategically, the United States plan of campaign did not take in Puerto Rico. The idea was to blockade Cuba, destroy the Spanish fleets in the Pacific and the Caribbean, then simply take over the islands. There could be no doubt about the outcome. Brave men manned the Spanish ships, as they had done since the days of the Conquistadores, but their war machinery was out of date and defective. When their Pacific fleet was attacked in Manila Bay at daybreak on April 30, it was little better than target practice for the Americans. The entire Spanish fleet and its supporting shore batteries were destroyed by noon, without the loss of a single American ship and with the wounding of only eight men. In the Caribbean, the Spanish ships escaped destruction by eluding the blockade of Cuba. American scout ships in hot pursuit of the Spaniards were the "ghosts" the Puerto Ricans had been seeing. On May 12, two days after the *Yale* incident these ghosts took on a more substantial form when American warships emerged from the early morning fog just off Morro Castle fortress and opened fire on the city of San Juan.

The bombing went on for three hours, and the people who lived in the higher sections of San Juan had to flee to Santurce. As in all wars, old men and women with children crowded the roads out of the city. Farmers who had been arriving for market abandoned their chickens and vegetables and fled.

From the safety of San Cristóbal, the Puerto Rican commander of the San Juan garrison, Captain Angel Rivero, watched this spectacle with quiet anger. "When I saw all those people," he wrote, "roused from their beds half-dressed by the American cannon and searching for safety in flight, I felt a profound hatred for those big ships and their immense superiority. God knows I tried, how I tried, to sink at least one. But halfway through the shelling I realized how pathetic our situation was, how wretched our artillery, how inexperienced our men, most of whom had never heard a cannon shot until that day. Then I cursed those men in Madrid who had left us defenseless and at the mercy of the enemy."

Rivero placed young Martin Cepeda, a Negro laborer who had volunteered to help, at the head of a dozen men. They were to bring ammunition from the battery of San Carlos, which was pointed toward land and therefore could not be used. While this operation was going on, a shell hit Cepeda, tearing his right arm to shreds.

Staggering to his feet, the young man cried: "Captain, I still have my other arm!" But a doctor had to amputate his shattered right arm on the spot, after which Rivero ordered Cepeda taken to a hospital. After the war was over, Cepeda was decorated by Spain.

There were other heroes and moments of heroism as the Spaniards tried desperately to defend Cuba and Puerto Rico, but for Spanish forces ashore and afloat there could be only one outcome. On July 3, the Spanish Caribbean fleet was nearly wiped out just off Santiago

Harbor. Two weeks later the city of Santiago itself surrendered, signaling the beginning of Cuba's liberation.

Hearing this news in Paris, the ailing revolutionary, Betances, wrote to a friend in New York: "What are the Puerto Ricans waiting for? Why are they not taking advantage of the war to rise? It is urgent that the American Army be received in Puerto Rico by Puerto Rican forces, flying the flag of independence. If Puerto Rico does not act soon, it will be forever an American colony."

In fact, on July 12, a manifesto *was* produced offering co-operation to the American forces in the liberation from Spanish rule. But that failed to satisfy either Betances or his fellow revolutionary, Hostos. They predicted that American intervention in Puerto Rico would have unforeseen consequences. "A national government cannot arrive in American ships," they warned, "it must already be there."

But in spite of these efforts, a mood of resignation had set in on the island. As always, there were differences of opinion. Barbosa, along with the entire Provisional Cabinet, had expressed support for the Spanish government during the crisis, and as a doctor, he had been in charge of one of the Red Cross districts, organized by Fernández Juncos in mid-April. During the shelling of San Juan, he had crossed the bay under fire to man his post at the hospital. But in spite of the war crisis, he and his deputies were just as stubborn as they had been before about accepting the election results and joining in the formation of the Insular Parliament.

Muñoz, on the other hand, argued that the Ameri-

cans must be faced with an accomplished fact. Even
if the United States annexed Puerto Rico and did not
give it independence, he believed that a functioning
autonomous government would be a bargaining point.
Muñoz took it for granted that the American democracy would be more liberal than monarchist Spain, and
would certainly allow autonomy to continue.

He was supported in this belief by Governor-General
Macías, and so on July 18, without the five protesting
barbosistas, the Insular Parliament began its sessions.
At the same time the new cabinet began to function;
it was headed by Muñoz and was made up entirely of
members of his own party. Then, having saved what he
could by creating an Insular Government, and unable
to change any further the course of events, Muñoz
waited for developments.

They were not long in coming. On July 21, a U.S. ex-
peditionary force under General Miles sailed from
Guantánamo, in Cuba, to invade Puerto Rico. Three
days later the ships sailed through the Mona Canal,
and with no lights showing, arrived in Guánica at dawn
on July 25. This was a small port on the southern coast
of the island, defended only by a lieutenant and eleven
men. After a brief exchange of fire, the lieutenant and
two of his men were badly wounded; the group retreated to Yauco, further inland. On the shore near
Guánica was a small wooden house with a zinc roof,
over which the Spanish flag was flying, and there at
nine o'clock that morning the Americans raised their
own flag and lowered the Spanish emblem.

By July 28, General Miles had taken possession of
Ponce, the most important city in the south, the Spaniards having retreated to San Juan. From his hotel

headquarters he issued a proclamation: "We have not come to make war upon the people of a country that for centuries has been oppressed, but, on the contrary, to bring you protection, not only to yourselves but to your property, to promote your prosperity, and to bestow upon you the immunities and blessings of the liberal institutions of our government."

When the Puerto Ricans heard this, their hopes were raised considerably. Certainly the behavior of the American troops as they moved northward was beyond reproach. They respected civilian life and property, and several placed flowers on the tombs of Spanish soldiers killed during the campaign, while American medical officers took care of the enemy wounded. Puerto Ricans were further impressed when a group of Catholic soldiers attended mass in Hormigueros.

It was clear that the Spaniards would not be able to defend San Juan. As the New York *Herald*'s correspondent reported, "The Spanish troops are sworn to fight. It is a heroic spectacle, since there is no hope for this handful of men, surrounded as they are by an enemy fleet, without any chance of reinforcements and already short of food and supplies." As the Spaniards were attempting to stop the Americans in the mountains near Aibonito, news of an armistice between the U.S. and Spain reached the troops. It was August 13. The Puerto Rican campaign had lasted just nineteen days.

General Ortega, the Spanish commander, made an effort to have the Americans recognize the existence of Puerto Rican sovereignty, as represented by Muñoz's autonomous government, but General Brooke, the American commander, could not do so because the armistice terms required that all political matters be

The last shots of the war were fired in the mountains near Aibonito.

handled by representatives of the two nations who were then meeting in Paris to decide peace terms. As a result only the military commissions were able to meet from September 10 to October 16, and Muñoz, disappointed again, realized that his "bargaining point" was not going to amount to much.

The arrangements for the transfer of sovereignty were simple. Ortega ended his role as Spanish commander, and placed Captain Rivero in charge. The transfer ceremony was planned in detail, and General Brooke sent an aide urging Muñoz Rivera to attend with all the members of his cabinet. They did so. By noon of October 18th, it was all over, and as of that day, General Brooke was the new governor of the island. His first decree set up military rule. It was printed in the *Gaceta,* the official government paper, which appeared for the first time with an American eagle on its masthead instead of the Spanish coat-of-arms. Later, on the afternoon of the eighteenth, all civilian officials of the Insular Parliament, from Muñoz Rivera on down, were required to sign a document renouncing allegiance to the Crown of Spain or any other state, and swearing to maintain and defend the Constitution of the United States.

So a new way of life began for Puerto Rico. With startling suddenness, the centuries-old quarrel with Spain was over. The U.S. had not granted independence, nor had it confirmed autonomy. The island was again a colony under military rule. From the promises General Miles had made, the Puerto Ricans were encouraged to hope for much, but they had been disappointed many times before. They waited to see if the promises would be fulfilled.

Chapter 9

No Independence

As 1898 drew to a close, Puerto Rico waited for the negotiators in Paris to decide its future. Until that was settled, the islanders had no choice but to accept military rule as the normal result of occupation, and hope it would be only a temporary matter.

On December 10, the news came from Paris. A treaty had been drawn up whose language made a striking distinction between Cuba and the other Spanish possessions—Puerto Rico, the Philippines, and other smaller islands in the Pacific and Caribbean. Spain gave up possession of Cuba, but it *ceded* the other islands to the United States. That meant Spain was no longer sovereign in Cuba, but neither was the United States. Occupation by American troops was simply permitted "under international law" for an unspecified time. However, the treaty gave to the United States outright sovereignty over Puerto Rico and the other possessions. Their future political status and the rights of their citizens were to be decided by the U. S. Congress.

By the middle of 1899, it was depressingly clear that everything was as it had been during the days before autonomy. Instead of a Spanish military officer in the governor's palace, there was an American general who ruled both military and civilian affairs. The old *incondicionales* were finished, but in their place sat the *barbosistas*, who were more willing to co-operate with the governor than the *muñocistas*, and so were the party favored by the Americans, just as the *incondicionales* had been favored by the Spanish authorities.

There the likeness ended, however. Even at its worst, American military rule was far better than Spanish rule. There was freedom of the press, freedom of association, and freedom of worship. Nor did these civil liberties depend on the inclination of those in power, as in Spanish days. They were rooted in the American system, even though Congress had not yet extended the Bill of Rights to the island. No longer could a man be sent to jail on mere suspicion. In the jails, reminders of the old, cruel days were removed—fetters, shackles, iron chains. Free public schooling was made compulsory, and free textbooks were provided. Schools were built; health services were given a great deal of fresh attention. Teams of American doctors arrived to help Puerto Rican doctors in the fight against yellow fever, malaria and other diseases which had afflicted the *jíbaros* for hundreds of years.

The economic situation was not quite as bright, on the other hand. The new credit and banking arrangements bankrupted many people. Free trade had ended, and coffee producers were hit hard because their chief markets, Spain and Cuba, were now lost to them. Worst of all, nearly all agricultural production had been brought to a standstill by the war, and thousands of field workers found themselves out of jobs. Most of the islanders felt by this time that their homeland, commercially speaking, was as badly off as it had been before 1812.

Military control was ended on April 12, 1900, when the Foraker Act, as it was known, was passed by the American Congress. It brought Puerto Rico under the monetary system and tariff provisions of the United

States, and set up free trade between the U.S. and the
island. Puerto Ricans were not to pay any federal taxes,
nor would they be expected to contribute in any way
to the American government under the historic principle of "no taxation without representation." But the act
provided no Bill of Rights, and the island's citizens
were not granted American citizenship. The United
States also continued to control the government of
the island, through a governor to be appointed by its
President, with the advice and consent of the U. S.
Senate.

All this was a disappointment to the Puerto Ricans.
It was a step backward from the Charter of Autonomy,
they agreed, and they began to talk of the charter as a
symbol of liberty, of Spanish rule as "the good old
days," and of the Spanish-American War as "a disaster."
It was even said that U.S. rule was illegal, because Puerto
Rico had never consented to the Treaty of Paris, and,
according to the Charter of Autonomy, no treaty affect-
ing the island was valid until approved by the Insular
Parliament.

None were more disappointed than Muñoz, Barbosa,
and de Diego, all of whom had fought to better Puerto
Rico, though in different ways. De Diego soon gathered around him those Puerto Ricans who were un-
happy with the new regime. Barbosa swallowed his
pride, put on a brave face, and held to his belief in
American democracy. Most Puerto Ricans followed him,
if for no better reason than lack of a choice, and his
party won the first two elections for the House under
the Foraker Act. What really puzzled de Diego and
his friends, however, was the action of the United
States in December 1902, when Cuba's American governor handed over administration to the island's first

elected President. Cuba was independent. What was the great difference, the de Diego faction wanted to know, between Cubans and Puerto Ricans? Why should Cuba be a sovereign nation and Puerto Rico a colony?

As for Muñoz, he sympathized with these feelings, but as a practical man he believed American rule was inevitable and the thing to do was to co-operate with it. However he came around more to de Diego's viewpoint as the island's economy continued to go down. More and more property owners were almost bankrupt, and more and more U.S. companies were taking advantage of the situation to buy off properties for the cultivation of sugar.

The Puerto Ricans bombarded Washington with appeals for help, but Congress did nothing and the citizens turned from Barbosa's moderation to de Diego's demands for independence. Muñoz, who was more and more active on de Diego's side, tried hard in Washington to get some consideration for Puerto Rico's case, but Congress was unwilling to listen. The United States government did not believe the islanders were really capable of ruling themselves. President William Howard Taft even thought the Puerto Ricans were being subversive by their show of independence and "rebellion."

Muñoz, seeing then that it would do no good to antagonize the Americans, began to work on them through more subtle pressures, trying to mobilize public opinion. He ran for Resident Commissioner in Washington, so that he could work more effectively, and was easily elected.

De Diego wanted no part of this middle-of-the-road approach. Independence, he declared, was the only an-

The jíbaros *lost their small coffee farms and were forced to work for unfair wages on the large sugar plantations.*

swer. Barbosa believed exactly the opposite. "The United States will never grant independence," he said, "but it might grant statehood if we live up to certain standards."

Muñoz cut through this debate with his usual common sense. "Statehood and independence are possibilities all right," he said, "but one should not waste time arguing and pondering over intangibles. One should get down to work and try to get the only thing possible at this time—some form of home rule. I know this is not perfect. For myself, I do not want to be an American inferior to other Americans. But anything is better than what we have now, so let's stop arguing and get to work."

It was not so easy to win the argument against de Diego, who had made the Unionista Party into something that was very close to being an Independence Party. The fight was a torture as far as Muñoz was concerned. In his heart he was for independence too, and de Diego was his friend. But a straight independence platform, as de Diego wanted, would handicap his position in Washington, and he felt forced to argue against it. He succeeded at last in toning down the platform's language, if nothing else.

Nevertheless, Muñoz went on working, with some result in 1917 when Congress passed the Jones Act, replacing the Foraker Act. This bill gave the Puerto Ricans a little more political freedom, and more important, contained the all-important Bill of Rights. At last, Puerto Ricans were granted American citizenship.

Muñoz did not live to see the act become law. After the House passed the bill, he was so ill that he had to return to Puerto Rico. He told his friends that he did not think the bill was perfect, but they realized that, as in the time of Sagasta, he had done all he could for the island. In November 1916, crowds carried his coffin from San Juan to Barranquitas, where he had been born, and there he was buried.

Passage of the Jones Act calmed the argument for a while, but unfortunately there was a political vacuum created by the death of Muñoz, followed by that of de Diego in 1918 and of Barbosa in 1921. The removal of this old generation of leaders, with no one to succeed them immediately, forced the political parties to face a period of readjustment.

Meanwhile, too, the United States entry into World War I in 1917 postponed any more decisions for the time being. The draft was extended to Puerto Rico, and 15,000 men showed their loyalty to their new citizenship by volunteering. In a few months, more than 17,000 Puerto Ricans were in training, of whom about 700 became officers. One of the instructors in the training camp was a Puerto Rican graduate of West Point, Luis Raúl Esteves.

In its early stages, the graduates of this camp were called the Puerto Rican Regiment, and were sent to reinforce troops guarding the Panama Canal. In later years it became the 65th Infantry Regiment, which distinguished itself in the Korean War. At home, civilians helped the war effort by buying bonds and contributing to the Red Cross. The American governor of Puerto Rico reported proudly in 1918: "Puerto Rico is using all the means at its disposal in helping to win the war."

After the war, the push for more freedom resumed, but again there was reluctance in Washington. President Calvin Coolidge seemed to be saying the same things President Taft had said, declaring that nothing had ever been promised to Puerto Rico by the Treaty of Paris. His words cast a shadow over relations between the two countries for years to come. What hurt most of all was the feeling Puerto Ricans had that the United States government looked down on them, as the Spanish government had not.

They were usually careful, however, to separate the *government* of the United States from American *individuals*. It was certainly not fair to say that the U.S. government intended to exploit Puerto Rico, yet it was estimated that only 15 per cent of the island's wealth was in the hands of Puerto Ricans. Two thirds of the profits from the sugar industry went out of the country to American-owned corporations. Construction of schools and roads, and health programs, were paid for not from direct United States economic aid, but from the island's budget. Salaries of American experts and civil servants also came out of local funds. As for the masses in the countryside, they had gained almost not at all from American prosperity.

The main reason for the island's difficulties was that it had finally become a sugar colony, a fate it had avoided for 400 years. Although the cultivation of sugar had increased during the 1800s, it was still second to coffee. But now the tariff regulations of the United States protected sugar, not coffee. By 1930, coffee made up less than 1 per cent of goods being sent out of the country, while sugar accounted for 60 per cent. And coffee is a poor man's crop. It can be raised on small farms and be picked by women and children.

Coffee farmers went out of business at a rapid rate, and their farms were picked up by American companies,

During the Depression in Puerto Rico, it was a common sight to see children in the streets who had lost their parents and had no place to go.

as were the lands of sugar farmers, who could not compete with the rich American corporations. American investors did not force anyone to sell, and they paid good prices for what they bought. However, after the deal was completed, since business opportunities were limited, the farmer spent his money bit by bit for living expenses, and in time found himself with neither land nor money.

When the Great Depression struck the United States in 1929, the effect was even worse in Puerto Rico. America had its hunger marches, bread lines, suicides, bank holidays, daily evictions, and bankruptcies, but Puerto Rico was harder hit because conditions were so much worse to begin with.

The politicians of the three existing parties, meanwhile, quarreled among themselves about what should be done. There was little to do but quarrel, since the real power was concentrated in the hands of Washington, the governor, and the sugar interests. Washington was unsympathetic and the sugar companies were certainly not interested in economic reform. As for the governors, it was altogether too much like the days of Spanish rule. Most of those appointed were chosen not for their ability, or their knowledge of local conditions, but simply as a reward for political services. Some of the American governors who sat in the ancient Spanish palace could not even speak Spanish. Surrounded by their aides, they came to symbolize American rule even more than the sugar companies did.

No wonder that talk of independence, which had subsided since the death of de Diego, began once more.

Chapter 10

New Leaders, New Politics

As the 1930s began, the political situation seemed much like that of the 1920s, except that there was more anti-American feeling. People still talked about the status of Puerto Rico. One politician said despairingly: "We go to sleep thinking about statehood, we develop insomnia thinking about independence, we get up in the morning thinking about autonomy. And all the time we forget the fundamental problems." The problems he meant were those of poverty.

But a breath of change blew into the political scene. Two new personalities appeared: Luis Muñoz Marín and Pedro Albizu Campos. Both men were to influence Puerto Rico, but their careers were to be very different.

Muñoz Marín, the son of Muñoz Rivera, would become the pilot of Operation Bootstrap, the economic development program which would change Puerto Rico from a stricken land to a prosperous community. Albizu Campos, who favored violence to win independence, died a broken man in 1965, after spending years in prison.

Operation Bootstrap put down its roots during the 1930s. It all started as the result of another quarrel about the question of independence. On one side was Albizu Campos, who saw Puerto Rico as an independent republic. Perhaps it could be associated with other Caribbean islands in a Federation of the Antilles, which would be free of U.S. control. There was nothing new about these proposals, but Albizu mixed with them expressions of intense hatred against everything of "Yankee origin." His constant demands for violent revolutionary action were a wide departure from Puerto Rico's political tradition of non-violence. He was no uneducated peasant revolutionary leader, however. Albizu was a brilliant man, with a Harvard law degree. In 1930, he was elected president of the Nationalist Party. It was a very small party, but anti-Americanism had grown so much that Albizu got attention far out of proportion to his job.

The main political parties were then the Unionistas, mostly pro-independence, and the Coalition, an alliance of several groups. For a time it looked as though the Nationalists would form an alliance with the Unionistas. Young Muñoz Marín proclaimed: "If the Unionista Party drops independence from its platform, I will vote for the Nationalists." Everyone noticed that Albizu was attracting crowds everywhere he went.

Many people were worried, however, about Albizu's constant calls for violence. Their suspicions of him were confirmed in April 1932, when a crowd which had just finished listening to one of Albizu's speeches marched on the Puerto Rican capitol building. As they marched, the crowd grabbed fence pickets, and brandishing them, shouted: "Long live the Republic!" They entered the capitol, where the legislature was in session. Police stopped them at the top of the stairs leading into the chamber, but in the scuffle that followed, one Nationalist was killed and several more wounded.

The Unionistas did not join with Albizu. Instead, the Party changed its name to the Liberal Party for the 1932 elections, and with its independence platform won the largest number of votes as a single party. Still, the combined votes of the Coalition parties were enough to make a majority and win the election. The Nationalist Party made a dismal showing; it polled only about 1 per cent of the vote and elected no candidates. Muñoz Marín was elected to the Senate as a Liberal. All things considered, the elections showed that although Puerto Ricans were stirred up about independence, they were unwilling to follow Albizu's tactics.

The results of the election that year in the United States proved to be far more important for Puerto Ricans than their own. Franklin Delano Roosevelt was elected, and a very different kind of President sat in the White House than had been there for a long time.

One of President Roosevelt's first non-domestic acts was to give to the island the same federal aid which had been given to states of the Union in the early years of the Depression. In August 1933, the operations of the Puerto Rico Emergency Relief Administration began. "La PRERA," as the islanders soon called it, spent about a million dollars a month, most of it on food and clothing, although it also encouraged public works in a limited way, and set up training programs in several skills. During its two years of operation, it kept alive about half the population of Puerto Rico and did much to improve the islanders' feeling about the United States.

But Muñoz did not want handouts to become a permanent fixture in the island. He began to lobby in Washington for a new federal money program in Puerto Rico. He had lived in that city with his father, had been educated in the United States, spoke perfect English, and knew many people who could help him. It was not surprising, then, that he was successful. He rallied support for an economic reconstruction program, drawn up by his friend Carlos Chardón, then Chancellor of the University of Puerto Rico. Chardón, a Cornell graduate, was an internationally recognized expert on agriculture. His proposals became known as the Chardón Plan, and were the basis for a new federal agency in 1935 called the Puerto Rican Reconstruction Administration. Its projects were far from being solutions to every problem, but the islanders were happy to know that someone was finally making an effort to reverse the process of decay which had been going on for so long, and because it was Muñoz who had made it possible, he became a national hero.

But the political opposition fought to discredit the new agency, and a fierce quarrel blazed up. Moreover, on a Sunday morning in February 1936, the American chief of police, Colonel E. Francis Riggs, unarmed, was coming out of San Juan Cathedral after mass when two young Nationalists rushed toward him and shot him dead. Nearly everyone on the island liked and respected Col. Riggs. Albizu had not taken part in the event, but his violent speeches had undoubtedly inspired it. He and seven other Nationalist leaders were sent to a federal prison for conspiring to overthrow the United States government.

(For years afterward, Albizu was in and out of jail, while he and his party carried on their campaign of terrorist violence. There were Nationalist attempts to kill many political leaders, including Muñoz Marín, in October 1950, when he was already governor of Puerto Rico. Two days later the terrorists made a daring attempt to assassinate President Harry S. Truman, and on March 1, 1954, four Nationalists invaded the House of Representatives in the American capital, sprayed it with bullets, and wounded five congressmen.)

Back in the 1930s the American reaction was to think that all Puerto Ricans who wanted independence were would-be assassins, and in turn the islanders, although most of them did not sympathize at all with the terrorists, were angered by the American reaction.

Tension was still high in April 1936 when events took a new twist. A bill was suddenly introduced in Congress by Senator Tydings providing for a yes-or-no vote by Puerto Ricans on the question of independence, which would be granted if a majority voted in favor. With independence abruptly thrust upon them in this way, Puerto Ricans found themselves not ready for it. The island's economy was tied solidly to the United States market and its tariff structure. This bill would simply cut the island loose. It offered no reasonable help for the readjustment of the economy. It seemed to the islanders that the United States, at the first sign of trouble, was trying to solve its "Puerto Rican problem" by simply getting rid of Puerto Rico. After a good deal of bitter political controversy, the Tydings bill was shelved. But the bill had started a feud in the Liberal Party between Muñoz, who had rejected it, and other Liberal leaders who had supported it. As a result, Muñoz was virtually banished from the party, and found himself at the head of a dissident group. Most people thought his career was finished. In Washington, too, he was out of favor, and at home he had only a few friends, no political organization, no political machine, and no money.

If Muñoz was in bad shape, so was Puerto Rico. The

Luis Muñoz Marín, former governor of Puerto Rico and pilot of Operation Bootstrap.

fervor of the New Deal had subsided in America, and with it programs were being changed and funds cut. Nationalist terrorism and the reaction to it had hastened that process where Puerto Rico was concerned. In fact, the "Puerto Rican New Deal" collapsed entirely. Out of these ruins, however, emerged the Popular Party and Operation Bootstrap.

Chapter 11

Operation Bootstrap—Success Today

Everybody in Puerto Rico today knows the story of Operation Bootstrap, so called because Muñoz Marín pulled up the island "by its bootstraps" to economic and political health. It has been the most publicized event in Puerto Rican history, and people still talk about it with pride.

The story begins in July 1938, when Muñoz and his little group of dissidents decided to form a new organization, the Popular Democratic Party. The established parties and the solid businessmen laughed at his efforts and said he would fail. Undiscouraged, Muñoz and his friends traveled from one end of the island to the other, collecting signatures to get the party registered in every town. Two years later, the amusement of the other parties turned into alarm when the Popular Democrats held the largest convention that had ever been seen. The new party astounded everyone when it drew up a platform which had nothing to say about political status. Since the days of Baldorioty no party had dared to avoid that question. Instead, Muñoz said clearly: "Status is not at issue. Social and economic justice is the issue."

This was really turning the traditional position upside down. The Popular Democrats were saying that Puerto Rico should straighten out its economy first, and after that it could think about its political status. It was said that Muñoz had decided to take this line while speaking to a group of *jíbaros* during the registration campaign.

While he talked about independence and national dignity and all the other ideas so dear to Puerto Rican politicians, he could not help observing the faces in his audience. They were the same faces he had described in 1925 for an American magazine: "These forsaken *jíbaros,* pale, frequently blond, always poverty stricken." Now he realized that the "big questions" he was talking about had little meaning for hungry men ridden by hookworm and malaria, and he decided it was more urgent to put these people back on their feet. Independence could wait. He coined a new fighting slogan for the *jíbaros,* "*Jalda arriba!*" meaning "Uphill we go!"

The campaign of the *populares* has since became a legend. Muñoz had scarcely enough money to support himself, much less to finance a party organization, and wealthy contributors were not at hand. The only way he could win was to get the free votes of the people. He could not even pay the two dollars the *jíbaros* usually got from politicians in exchange for their votes.

But Muñoz would not have wanted to buy votes in any case. He did not want people to vote for money. He wanted people to vote because they understood the issues and what their vote could accomplish. He tried to tell them these things, traveling everywhere in a battered car wearing no coat or tie, explaining to the poor in simple language what he meant to do. This intellectual man wrote poetry in his spare time, but when he talked to the voters, it was in their language. His friends did the same. In towns and rurals areas a *popular* could always be found patiently explaining to his listeners how a man could use the vote to improve his life.

When the returns began to come in on election day,

the results electrified everyone. Muñoz's friends ran to each other shouting, "We've won! We've won! The *jíbaros* didn't sell their vote! We've won!" Muñoz, it is said, had tears in his eyes. The *jíbaros* were starving, but they had not let him down.

Washington was stirred by Muñoz's astonishing triumph, although its official reaction was not yet certain. The first response was to send down Rexford Guy Tugwell to look the situation over and make a report. Tugwell had been an important figure in the Roosevelt administration from the beginning, and had once been Secretary of Agriculture, so he was considered a good man to make the assessment. After studying the Muñoz programs, his report was a recommendation to Washington that the governor sign the bills creating them. A year later, Tugwell himself became governor—the last American governor Puerto Rico was to have.

Muñoz's Land Law established an agency to purchase land from the sugar corporations, and since small holdings could not make money in the sugar industry, the government was to administer these lands. The government was therefore the employer. The workers were not only to get wages but also were to share in the profits. Other lands were to be divided into small lots and sold to farmers, who could buy them on easy terms from the government. Agencies were set up to take care of housing projects, co-operatives, and credit unions. Power plants were to be built and electricity brought to the rural areas. A Central Planning Board was formed to avoid duplication and waste.

Puerto Rico was very much underdeveloped at the time of Muñoz's victory, but it no longer is, and its progress toward becoming an industrialized area is often studied by other planners in countries which are going through the same process.

The Planning Board began by buying off some of the sugar industry's holdings with money from the island's budget. The profits made from the sugar crop, plus more budget money, were used to build a few plants. At that point, however, difficulties came up. The government could not get enough capital to make a difference. Great sums were needed to industrialize the island—sums in the billions. And this in a country whose budget dealt only in millions. Besides, skilled men were scarce, sales management was not efficient, and the few existing plants had begun to lose money instead of making profits.

The planners asked themselves, "Who has plenty of capital and know-how, and can keep a factory going?" There was an obvious answer: "American businessmen." That was how the second stage of Operation Bootstrap began.

At first the problem was how to talk American businessmen into transferring some of their operations to Puerto Rico. Americans were in business to make profits, not to make gifts to the government of Puerto Rico. The island could not expect to get something for nothing. It would have to make exchanges which would bring benefit to both sides.

So the planners moved to the next question: What did Puerto Rico have to offer? For one thing, it had an available labor supply. Unlike most other underdeveloped countries, Puerto Ricans were not engaged in subsistence farming, and so they did not have to be taken out of food production to work in factories. In any case, the island was already importing most of its food from the United States. The unemployed, then, were an advantage, not a liability. They formed a ready-made supply of labor which could be trained for light industry, and since the United States minimum wage laws did not apply to the island, they could work for less money than Americans.

This wage difference was not enough, however, to attract American businesses in large numbers. Wages could not be too low, or the Puerto Ricans would find themselves being taken advantage of all over again, this time by the Americans in collaboration with their own island government. The planners decided that various kinds of businesses which relocated in the island would not have to pay taxes. That in itself was a strong argument for relocation.

The search for American investors began in earnest. A special agency (Fomento) was formed just for that purpose, and a young pharmacist from Ponce named Teodoro Moscoso was placed in charge of it. Moscoso worked in New York and began to cultivate businessmen. The result was a rush of American companies, big and small, into Puerto Rico. The goods produced ranged from chemicals to electrical instruments to textiles. There were a few failures, but most of the investors succeeded and remained even after their tax exemption privileges were over. There was plenty of inducement to stay besides making money; Puerto Rican sun, sea, and skies were hard to beat.

As time went on and industrialization proceeded, wages rose until today the annual per capita income of the island is the highest in Latin America. When Operation Bootstrap began, it was about $140; it is now more than $1000. The annual rate of growth in Puerto

Puerto Ricans formed a ready-made supply of labor for U.S. businesses interested in setting up their industries in Puerto Rico.

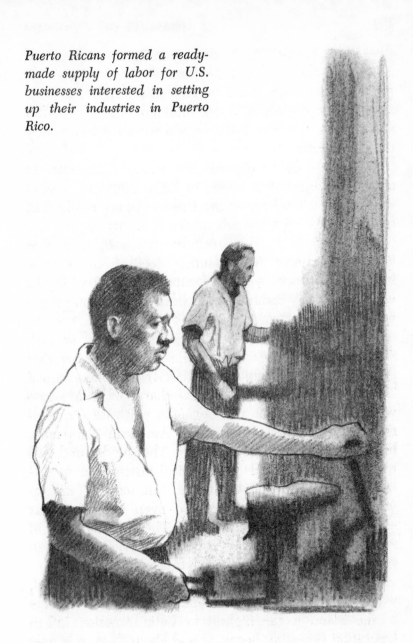

Rico today is about 6 per cent, as compared with about 3 per cent in the United States, about 2 per cent in Mexico, and about 4 per cent in Israel.

The island can be considered industrialized today because a little more than half its income comes from manufacturing, not agriculture. Sugar is still important, but it makes up only about one fifth of the island's income. More sugar is being produced than ever before, but there are many other commodities so the percentage falls.

One effect of Puerto Rico's "economic miracle" was to demolish the idea that tropical countries cannot industrialize. It must be remembered, however, that American investment could not do it all; it had only produced a sugar colony before. It was the Puerto Ricans themselves who found the ways and means to use American capital for the benefit of both countries, and it was they who were willing to be trained and to work.

All of this, however, meant the overturning of old ideas, and it was not easy. At the beginning, when Muñoz did not command a large majority, the opposition continued to obstruct his projects. There were others, too, who had higher motives than political ones for their opposition. These people, often members of Muñoz's own party, still wanted some action taken for independence. They worried about the increasing Americanization of the island, and they did not want Puerto Rico to lose its national identity.

Muñoz refused to give in to those in favor of independence, and they had to form their own party. He went after his objectives in a straight line, and kept insisting: "The object is that no one become a beggar or a slave to extreme poverty. What must be done to save Puerto Rico must be done under whatever political status."

Some political gains were made. When Governor Tugwell resigned in 1946, President Truman appointed Jesús Piñero to take his place—the first Puerto Rican ever to hold the office. Shortly after, Congress passed a bill making the office of governor elective. In 1948, Muñoz Marín became the first elected governor in the island's history, taking office on January 2, 1949. The celebrations for his inaguration broke as many records as the first convention of the Populares.

After his election, Muñoz worked for some arrangement that would end Puerto Rico's colonial status. The result of his renewed lobbying in Washington was Public Law 600, approved in July 1950. This law, said Congress, was "in the nature of a compact so that the people of Puerto Rico may organize a government pursuant to a constitution of their own adoption."

The law was presented for approval in 1951 to Puerto Rican voters, who voted 3 to 1 to accept it. In the same year a convention was elected to draw up the constitution called for by the law. This was ready in February 1952, and in March the voters approved it overwhelmingly in a special referendum. In turn, a joint resolution in Congress approved it in July 1952, and President Truman signed it into law.

A few days later, on July 25, Muñoz issued a formal proclamation of the new Constitution and the changes in status it called for. Henceforth Puerto Rico was to be known officially as an Estado Libre Associado, or Commonwealth, a unique arrangement in law between a ruling power and a dependency. The United States was to continue to take care of defense, the post office,

Through hard work and the will to survive, Puerto Ricans have pulled themselves by their bootstraps out of a poverty which had existed for more than 400 years.

and several other agencies functioning on the island, as it did in the States. The economic provisions of the Foraker and Jones acts remained unchanged. The island would still have a Commissioner Resident in Washington, but it would have its own constitution, its own elected officials, and control over local affairs.

Since this was such a flexible arrangement, international lawyers are still arguing about the meaning of the phrase "Free Associated State." Whatever it means, it works. More changes may come. At the present time the island has a very strong, active pro-statehood party, while the Independentists are in the minority.

Puerto Rico's fundamental problem remains an economic one. The industrialization program is not over. There is still unemployment, and Puerto Ricans still migrate to the United States in large numbers, searching for jobs. Skilled workers are still hard to get. Puerto Rico needs more engineers, technicians, and management people who can speak both Spanish and English. The slogan continues to be, *"Jalda arriba!"*

Nearly seventy years ago the great historian of the island, Salvador Brau, concluded his history of Puerto Rico with the American occupation and these words: "It is up to the people of Puerto Rico to start anew."

Since then, Puerto Ricans have not only started anew but they have made their country a model for emerging nations. They have pulled themselves by their bootstraps out of a poverty which had existed for more than four hundred years. Their greatest asset is still the attitude that enabled them to do it, and in this is the best promise for their future.

Index

Africa, slaves from, 11–12, 21, 33, 39

Agriculture (farmers and farming), 20–21, 22, 29, 31–34, 49–50 (See also Coffee; Sugar); Operation Bootstrap and, 100, 101, 104; U.S. rule and, 81, 88–90, 100, 104

Agüebaná, 6–8, 13

Aibonito, 77, 78

Aid programs, 93–94, 100–8

Albizu Campos, Pedro, 91–92, 93; death of, 91; imprisoned for terrorism, 94

Alfonso, King of Spain, 59

Amézquita, Juan de, 37

Añasco, 38

Andino brothers, 38

Antilles, 5, 91. See also Caribbean

Apricots, 36

Aragon, Sancho de, 21

Arawak Indians, 5–8, 9–19

Arecibo, 5, 31; repels English invasion attempt, 38

Art, 62

Asimilistas, 55, 60

Assembly, P.R., 67. See also Legislature, P.R.

Association for the Abolition of Slavery, 50, 51

Autonomist Party, 60–61, 62–69, 70; founded by Baldorioty, 60–61

Autonomy, 55–69, 76–97 passim, 105–8 (See also specific individuals, parties); charter granted, 67–69

Aymamón, 6

Baldorioty de Castro, Rámon, 55–56; reorganizes liberals and founds new Autonomist Party, 60–61

Barbosa, José Celso, 60, 62, 69, 75, 83; reorganizes Autonomists, 64; death of, 87; and Pure Autonomists (barbosistas), 67–69, 70, 75–76, 80; and U.S. rule, 82, 83

Barbosistas, 67–69, 70, 75–76, 80

Barranquitas, 87

Bayamón, 62

Becerrillo, 21

Benitez, José Gautier, 62

Benito, Don, 35–36

Betances, Ramón, 51, 54, 75

Bill of Rights, 81, 82, 86

Biminí, 19

Bohíos, 31

Bootstrap, Operation, 91, 96, 97, 98–108

Borinquen, 3–8, 9–19

Botello, Andrés, 37

Brau, Salvador, 65–66

Brooke, John R., 1, 77–79

Business development, 101–4

Cabinet, Parliamentary, 68, 76, 79

Cabo Rojo, 47

Caciques, 5–8, 13–18; Supreme, 5

Cádiz, 44

Caguas, 5

Canal Zone, 4, 87

Cangrejos, 34, 38–40

Cannibalism, 21

Canóbanos, 5

Caparra, 15, 16, 17